An Asian Theology
of Liberation

FAITH MEETS FAITH

An Orbis Series in Interreligious Dialogue

Paul F. Knitter, General Editor

In our contemporary world, the many religions and spiritualities stand in need of greater intercommunication and cooperation. More than ever before, they must speak to, learn from, and work with each other, if they are to maintain their own vitality and contribute to a better world.

FAITH MEETS FAITH seeks to promote interreligious dialogue and cooperation by providing a forum for exchange between followers of different religious paths, making available to both the scholarly community and the general public works that will focus and give direction to this emerging encounter among the religions of the world.

Already published:

Toward a Universal Theology of Religion, Leonard Swidler, Editor
The Myth of Christian Uniqueness, John Hick and Paul F. Knitter, Editors

FAITH MEETS FAITH SERIES

An Asian Theology of Liberation

Aloysius Pieris, S.J.

ORBIS BOOKS

Maryknoll, New York 10545

First published in book form as *Theologie der Befreiung in Asien: Christentum im Kontext der Armut und der Religionen*, in 1986, by Herder Verlag, Herman-Herder-Strasse 4, 7800 Freiburg im Breisgau.

Published by Orbis Books, Maryknoll, NY 10545
Published in the United Kingdom by T & T Clark
Manufactured in the United States of America

Manuscript editor and indexer: William E. Jerman

LIBRARY OF CONGRESS
Library of Congress Cataloging-in-Publication Data

Pieris, Aloysius.
  An Asian theology of liberation / Aloysius Pieris.
    p. cm.—(Faith meets faith series)
  Bibliography: p.
  Includes index.
  ISBN 0-88344-627-8. ISBN 0-88344-626-X (pbk.)
    1. Liberation theology. 2. Christianity—Asia. 3. Asia—
Religion. 4. Christianity and other religions. I. Title.
II. Series: Faith meets faith.
BT83.57.P54 1988
230'.2—dc19
                            88-1783
                             CIP

To my parents
Walter John Pieris (1887–1966)
and
Dona Anselmina Setunga (1897–)

Contents

vii

Foreword

In the essays that make up this volume, Aloysius Pieris confronts two of the most urgent, complex, and therefore promising questions that face the Christian religion—or any religion—today. They are questions that engage both mind and heart, and disturb both intellect and conscience—questions that shake the foundations of Christianity's self-image and its truth claims: the question of the *many poor* and the question of the *many religions.*

It will not take the reader long to feel how both these questions vibrate within each of the following essays; they are the stuff out of which Pieris fashions his proposal for Asian theology of liberation. In his view, the answers that the Christian churches give to the challenge of the many poor and the many religions will determine the relevance of Christianity in Asia. The same would be true, one suspects, for the relevance of Christianity anywhere in our contemporary world.

Pieris finds himself in a situation where he has no choice but to face these two issues. As he reaches out into the Asian context from his study center in Gonawala, Sri Lanka, he is met by the realities of Asian poverty and Asian religiousness. In this context—in his outrage at the injustices wrought upon his people and in the native bonds he feels with his people's religions—he has come to realize not only that Christianity must respond to *both* these issues, but that it must respond to both of them *together.* Herein lies the creativity and the challenge of Pieris's thought—in the way he argues, from a variety of perspectives, that Christians will not adequately address the problem of Asian poverty unless they do so within the context of dialogue with Asian religions, and that they will not carry on an authentic and successful interreligious encounter unless they base that dialogue on a concern for the poor. Asian theology of liberation will take shape out of a Christian dialogue with Asian religion. Dialogue and liberation call out to each other.

In making his case—which he does with both clarity and passion—Pieris poses sharply honed challenges to different sectors of Christian theology and church practice, as well as to followers of other religious ways. His fellow Christians in North America and Europe, as well as in Latin America, will find this book not only insightful and creative but challenging and disturbing. Pieris will rattle or revamp some of their deepest convictions and most cherished commitments.

There are five audiences for whom his vision is particularly pertinent and disturbing:

1. To *advocates of interreligious dialogue and pluralism,* Pieris voices the "hermeneutical suspicion" that perhaps all their conferences, their scholarly and mystico-ritual encounters, might be serving as a holy smoke screen behind

which they are avoiding, unconsciously, the harsh realities of poverty, injustice, and exploitation—and perhaps even their own religious complicity in such realities. Is dialogue being practiced on mountaintops by a privileged holy remnant of scholars and mystics, while the masses are left in the valleys to dialogue with malnutrition and disease and lack of land? More incisively, Pieris asks whether the West is now importing the raw materials of Eastern spiritualities, refashioning them into privatistic, personal-growth products, and offering nothing in return. For Pieris, interreligious dialogue that does not come out of an experience of human suffering, and does not explore the this-worldly, liberative message of all religions, is a violation of the very nature of religion and of interreligious dialogue. He does not mince words.

2. For *liberation theologians*, especially Latin American, Pieris has both words of wholehearted endorsement and gratitude as well as words of admonition and invitation to broaden their views. These pages will make clear that, with his Latin American mentors, Pieris understands "liberation" not as an adjective but as a synonym for "theology." Yet he poses a fundamental question for his mentors: Is their vision of the kingdom of God perhaps too narrow because it is too Christian? Have the Latin American (and North American) liberationists been too much influenced by the two "mighty Karls" of dialectical fame—Marx, whose dialectical materialism failed to see that there is indeed *revolution* in religion, and Barth, whose dialectical theology failed to see that there is *revelation* in religion? And because of this narrow view of other religions, because many Christian liberation theologians ignore the "soteriological nucleus" or the "prophetico-political resources" of other religions, they have, perhaps unwittingly, been keeping these Asian religious traditions in Western bondage.

More positively, Pieris invites Christian liberationists to open their vision and their praxis to the revelation of profound, perhaps perplexing, religious truth in other traditions—truth that has much to offer for the transformation and liberation of this world. Even for purely pragmatic reasons, Christians working in Asia must accept this invitation, for, Pieris admonishes, concientización (liberative conscientization) will not work for the majority of Asian poor unless it is couched in and inspired by the symbols and beliefs of their own religious world. At least in Asia, what is needed, therefore, are not "base Christian communities," but "base human communities," in which, for instance, Buddhists and Christians will come together on the basis of their shared concern for and praxis of liberation—and on this basis they will understand themselves and each other ever more deeply and engagingly.

Concerning what Christians might actually learn from Buddhists in this joint effort for liberation, Pieris merely mentions in this volume what he has developed elsewhere (and what will be contained in his coming work on Christian-Buddhist dialogue): that integral liberation will be realized only through a paradoxical joining of the Christian insistence on the priority of agapeic praxis with the Buddhist insistence on the priority of gnostic wisdom. In addition, Christian sociological analysis of imposed poverty needs to be linked with Buddhist psychological analysis and voluntary poverty. The fruits of dialogue, if gathered among the poor, are abundant.

3. For *contemporary "liberal" theologians* who have developed a Christian theology of religions, Pieris asks whether they might be too uncritical of another mighty "Karl" of this century. Rahner's progressive theological response to non-Christian religions inspired the Second Vatican Council's declaration on other religions and has permeated Christian views of other faiths during the past decades. Rahner clearly moved Christian theology of religions from the exclusivist position of "Christ-against-the-religions" toward the inclusivist attitude of "Christ-of-the-religions." Liberal Christians now recognize the value of other religions as genuine bearers of revelation and as "legitimate" ways of salvation. Pieris affirms all this—but then goes on to pose the prodding question whether these liberal views are proposing a "crypto-colonialist theology of religions." For instance, their theories of "anonymous Christianity" can be cancelled by counterclaims of "anonymous Hinduism." If Christians look upon Buddha as a precursor for Christ, they must allow Buddhists to regard Jesus as a bodhisattva who has not yet realized Buddhahood.

So Pieris suggests that what is "absolute" in Jesus is not to be found in titles such as "Christ" or "Son of God," but in the saving mystery of salvation/liberation that Jesus communicates in his person and in his teaching—and which is recognized in other religions and named differently. For Asian theologians, in Pieris's estimation, the issue of the uniqueness of "Christ," as traditionally understood, is a non-issue. The theology of religions he has worked out in the context of an Asian theology of liberation makes room for a genuine Christian recognition of religious pluralism, without slipping down the slopes of relativism.

4. For the *Asian Christian churches* Pieris raises another issue that has proven to be not only delicate but explosive. He boldly asserts that the Christian churches *in* Asia have not yet really become churches *of* Asia. An authentic, deep-reaching process of inculturation by which Western Christianity becomes Asian Christianity has *not* taken place—and the reason, paradoxically, has been because of the excessive or misdirected stress that the churches have placed on *inculturation*. From Pieris's experience and perspective, all the conferences, books, and efforts toward inculturation have to a great extent distracted the churches from the "colossal scandal of institutionalized misery that poses a challenge to every religion." Efforts and concerns to take on the *culture* of Asia have been a blinder to or an escape from the need to confront the *poverty* of Asia. Pieris, as it were, turns the tables on the inculturationist question and insists that it is precisely by identifying with Asian peoples in their struggle for justice—as that struggle is nourished by their traditional religions—that authentic inculturation will take place and the church *in* Asia will indeed become the church *of* Asia. Inculturation, therefore, cannot be separated from liberation.

Liturgy provides Pieris with a concrete example of why inculturation has failed and how it might succeed. Since Vatican II there has been no true liturgical renewal in Asia—nor, Pieris argues, in the church in general—because liturgy has been understood primarily as "church liturgy" rather than as "liturgy of life." Liturgy has been practiced and taught mainly as an inner-church reality, as in itself "the source and summit" of Christian life (Vatican II), rather than as an engagement with life and a struggle for humanization, which *then* calls for and needs ritual-symbolic expression and strengthening within church liturgies. Liturgy has been too apolitical and therefore has not grown out of the life and culture of Asia. Pieris reminds his fellow Christians that the first liturgy on Calvary did not take place in the temple and therefore was not a church liturgy; it took place outside the temple, in the midst of human life, human struggles.

5. For his *fellow believers in Eastern religions, especially Buddhism*, Pieris also has some challenging claims. Although he clearly rejects the widespread academic pigeonholing of the so-called "Eastern religions" (Pieris calls them gnostic religions) as other-worldly and the so-called "Western religions" (agapeic religions in Pieris's vocabulary) as this-worldly spiritualities, and although he finds in *all* religions a denunciation of a world order built on the "mammon values" of greed and the accumulation of wealth, he suggests to his "Eastern" religious companions that there is something distinctive about the bibilical God, something that is not found so clearly expressed in non-Semitic religions. In the Jewish-Christian Bible we witness not only an irreconcilable antagonism between God and mammon but also an *irrevocable covenant between God and the poor.* The God of Moses and of Jesus shows a special preference for slaves and all those who have been deprived of life by other human beings. Indeed, the biblical understanding of the covenant between God and the poor is such that it leads to a nondualistic understanding/experience of the liberative activity of God and the liberative activity of the poor as "one indivisible Saving Reality." Transcendent divine Reality is realized as immanent within human liberative activity. Here, perhaps, Buddhism and other Eastern spiritualities may have something to learn (just as Christianity has much to learn from them in other areas). This is a suggestion that Pieris develops more amply in the companion volume to follow this one.

In his *Asian Theology of Liberation*, Pieris combines the clarity and care of an academician with the passion and daring of a prophet. Orbis Books is happy and honored to include this volume in its "Faith Meets Faith Series" and to make Aloysius Pieris's thought available to a broader English-reading public. His Asian voice, issuing from his local culture and his local church in Asia, has much to say to the universal Christian church and to the universal concern for human betterment.

Paul F. Knitter
Xavier University, Cincinnati

Preface

The Second Vatican Council was for me a point of departure rather than a point of arrival, as I joined my Asian colleagues over twenty years ago in the challenging task of applying the conciliar teachings to our Asian context and of trying to give concrete Asian form to the spirit of the Council. We did this in three different ways: (1) by participating in the *Asian reality,* (2) by celebrating our discoveries *liturgically*, and (3) finally, by reflecting *theologically* on both these experiences. The articles gathered in this volume represent only the third area of my activity: theological reflection.

It was of course impossible to include in these pages all of the sixty or more articles written during the two post-conciliar decades, most of which are listed in the bibliography appended to this book. Only nine pieces have been selected for this volume, and they are assembled here in a thematic order so as to bring out more clearly both the theological mood and the theological method that guided me when writing them.

The chapters that make up parts 2 and 3 of this volume, which offer the main elements of my thinking, present my own perspectives on the "inculturationist" versus "liberationist" debate among Asian Christian theologians. In order to set these issues in a more substantive context, three chapters on spirituality, poverty, and liberation comprise part 1. I think they provide a helpful introduction to the entire book.

There is, however, a serious lacuna in this collection. Though I have made explicit reference to feminist concerns in passing, I have lamentably failed to integrate these concerns into my analysis of oppression in the Third World. As my students will testify, the feminist issue has been a central and pervasive theme in my annual lectures at the East Asian Pastoral Institute in Manila since 1973. Yet the absence of this issue in my writings points to a serious negligence on my part, which, with the help of my feminist friends and critics, I hope to remedy in the near future.

This volume owes its existence to the ground-laying work done for the German edition by my friend and confrere Ludwig Wiedenmann, S.J., of the Missiological Institute in Aachen and to the persistent encouragement and assistance lavished on me by the Orbis editorial staff, together with Paul Knitter of Xavier University in Cincinnati. They all thought that what I have learned from my Asian experience would be of value to readers in Europe and North America. To all these friends I extend a sincere word of appreciation and gratitude.

Aloysius Pieris, S.J.
Tulana Research Center
Gonawala-Kelaniya
Sri Lanka

xv

PART I

Poverty and Liberation

1

Spirituality in a Liberative Perspective

The Second Vatican Council opened the door for a comprehensive definition of what has traditionally been compartmentalized as liturgy, spirituality, and secular (that is, socio-political) commitment. Yet because of an unhappy juxtaposition of old formulas and new perspectives, a trichotomy persists between the sacramental, the contemplative, and the active (or activist) dimensions of Christian "spirituality."

In the conservative stream of thinking, which includes some recent pronouncements of the official church, there is a tendency to take a narrow view of contemplation as spirituality par excellence, if not also as spirituality per se, without which "liturgy" and more especially the Christian "commitment" to the paschal transformation of the world would be unspiritual.

It is this mode of perceiving "spiritual life" that invariably reduces the trichotomy to a triple dichotomy, namely:

(a) liturgy versus spirituality,
(b) spirituality versus secular involvement,
(c) secular involvement versus liturgy.

The refusal to see all these three elements as mutually inclusive dimensions of one authentic Christian life creates an insoluble circularity in all the attempts made so far to overcome any given "spiritual crisis," as will be illustrated below. It is here that liberation theology introduces a healthy synthesis by identifying the exact locus where these three aspects overlap. This it does by refocusing the church's attention on:

(a) the liturgy of life,
(b) the theology of the cross, and
(c) the historical Jesus and his humanity.

All three themes are actually three different modes of perceiving the same mystery of redemption.

However, no Latin American theologian should be held responsible for the peculiar manner in which I formulate the problem of spirituality as it exists in the contemporary church or for the framework (of the "triple dichotomy")

Originally a contribution to *Vida y Reflexión* (Lima, 1984), a collection of articles published to commemorate the tenth anniversary of the publication of Gustavo Gutiérrez' *Theology of Liberation*. First published in English in *The Month*, 16 (1983) 118–24.

3

within which I have tried to perceive, clarify, and appreciate whatever liberation theology has contributed toward the theology of spirituality. This presentation, therefore, reflects my own personal assessment of the ever-new and yet
ever-ancient principles of spirituality that seem to be emerging from the
ecclesial life of basic communities in Latin America.

LITURGY VERSUS SPIRITUALITY

Focus on the Liturgy of Life

Let me begin with the analysis of the first dichotomy—namely, the one
between liturgy and spirituality. During the five decades that preceded the
Second Vatican Council, two parallel solutions to this problem were offered in
the course of the well-known Jesuit-Benedictine controversies on spirituality.
The 1917 *Codex Juris Canonici* emphasized the ritual, juridical, external, and
hierarchically controllable elements of Christian worship. Theological manuals later extended this notion to ludicrous extremes, defining liturgy as the
merely sensible, ceremonial, and ornamental part of Catholic worship (Nava-
tel) or as a set of ecclesiastical controls over the performances of public worship
(Callewaert). No wonder the Jesuits wanted to supplement liturgy with a
personal, contemplative spirituality and thus deritualize it.

The Benedictine school, led by Beauduin (following Guéranger of the nineteenth century), tried to salvage the notion of liturgy from its overritualistic
connotation by redefining it as the *ecclesial* (presumably not ecclesiastical)
continuation of the Christ-Mystery, participation in which constitutes true
spirituality. In their critique of Ignatian spiritual exercises, some Benedictines
insisted that a spirituality that is not liturgical is not ecclesial either (in which
case, how could it even be Christian?). Liturgy was none other than the exercise
of the priesthood of Christ—that is, of the total Christ, head and members.
Spirituality, then, is not a prelude or an accompaniment or a supplement to
liturgy but is itself coextensive with liturgy or Christian worship. One could say
that the Jesuits brought in a personal dimension to what they regarded as a
collective "rite," whereas the Benedictines restored an ecclesial character to an
otherwise individualistic "spirituality." The Benedictines won the day.

This new understanding of liturgy found its way into the encyclical *Mediator
Dei* (1947) lock, stock, and barrel. From there, it was just one step to the
Liturgical Constitution of Vatican II, thanks to the intervening decade and a
half of "reforms" enacted from the top and "renewal" erupting from the base
of the church. *Sacrosanctum Concilium* of Vatican II did not hesitate to claim
that the liturgy was the "source and summit" (*fons et culmen*) of Christian
existence. Never before has a more thorough integration of spirituality and
liturgy been advocated by the official church.

Thus, when the Liturgical Constitution was triumphantly voted in at the
council, there was an explicit hope among liturgists that *liturgical* renewal
would turn out to be a *spiritual* renewal of the church. But an honest assess-

ment of the two postconciliar decades has another story to tell. The conciliar *Instructiones* were often interpreted and executed with a preconciliar rubrical mentality. The Roman Curia failed to make the "paradigm shift" from the canonical definition of liturgy to the conciliar understanding of worship. And many renewalists were busy moving altars, introducing vernacular texts, composing new prayers and songs, simplifying vestments, improving on gestures, and so on, with the result that liturgy often became a new series of words and activities that prevented the Word from speaking and acting sacramentally within the community.

Contrary to the conciliar teaching on liturgy, what happened was often a change of *rite*, and not a change of *life*. And once the new rite lost its novelty, the church was back to square one. Soon spirituality had to be once again imported from outside to vivify the liturgy! Charismatic renewal and oriental mysticism invaded the Western church, reinforcing not only the personal but also the traditionally apolitical character of both spirituality and liturgy! As regards the nexus between liturgy and spirituality, the Latin church slipped back into the old dualism. In this particular respect, the post-Vatican situation, contrary to expectation, was only a little better than the post-Tridentine period when the liturgy used to be supplemented by numerous devotions and "spiritualities"!

Why do we continually fall into this rut? Why this circularity? In my view, the reason might be this: the Roman church has, somewhere in the course of its history, devalued the most crucial dimension of spirituality—the *liturgy of life*, which is the matrix of all sacramental expressions, for it is the context of a living encounter with God in Christ. Sacramental life and mysticism cannot be artificially reconciled if they are both uprooted from their natural environment, which is the paschal Mystery of Christ continued in the (secular) lives and struggles, in the deaths and triumphs of his members—for Christ dies, not in the temple, the place of traditional liturgies, but outside it, and *ubi Christus ibi ecclesia* (where Christ is, there is the church)—not necessarily the other way about. Wherever the paschal Mystery is enacted today, there Christ is united to his loyal members; it is there that the *real* church is gathered; there the *true* liturgy takes place; there, *authentic* spirituality is lived—for in victimhood lies the exercise of the priesthood of Christ.

Thus it is in the rise of basic communities in Latin America that one begins to observe this kind of mutual enveloping of liturgy, spirituality, and secular action, constituting a genuine renewal of the church. This is liberation theology in practice. It could not have come *directly* from Vatican II, though Vatican II prepared the ground for it by creating an ethos of theological freedom and ecclesiological pluralism.

Vatican II is undoubtedly the most significant achievement, in recent times, of the Western patriarchate in renewing its life within its own tradition. It was trying to break away from a legalistic outlook to a *liberal* one; from lapsarian pessimism to a theology of *hope*; from an ecclesiastical narcissism to an adventurous involvement with the *world*. Its most conciliar document,

Gaudium et Spes (proposed and prepared at the council itself), contains precious new perspectives, and has initiated a far-reaching dialogue with the *modern* world. But this modern world, on close scrutiny, seems to be primarily the First World, the Western technocratic world spreading its tentacles over the entire globe—not the *unjust* world created in the very process of building that modern world! Even the highly dangerous missiology of developmentalism, which corrupted Third World churches with neocolonialist triumphalism, seems to have received tacit approval in the conciliar document on missions (*Ad Gentes*, chaps. 1 and 2). This contradicts other healthier perspectives opened up in *Lumen Gentium* and *Gaudium et Spes*. Vatican II fostered in the West a liberal theology, not a liberation theology; a progressive theology, not a radical theology.

The Western church's widespread overreaction both for and against the encyclical *Humanae Vitae* of Paul VI, and its comparative indifference to his *Populorum Progressio*, is an index of this situation. Why? Because its liberalist preoccupation with individual moral freedom is not sufficiently rooted in the liberational zeal for the total human freedom of oppressed peoples. In the first encyclical, which deals with birth control, the pope resisted the modern world's technological manipulation of human life, and in the second encyclical, which deals with justice, he acknowledged the diabolical extent to which this manipulation goes on in the Third World. Progressive theologians failed to realize that the pharaohs who govern this modern world are overeager to reduce the birth rate of their slaves whose numbers are indeed a threat to their comfort and security. The Latin American response was different. It was there that *Populorum Progressio* was taken seriously, because local churches recognized the injustice lurking behind the veil of modernity, the inequalities riding on the waves of technocratic "progress," and the greed for "wealth control" hiding behind the zeal for birth control. No wonder they gave us Medellín—and then, liberation theology.

To grasp the difference between these two perspectives, one must return to the earliest Christian understanding of liturgy, spirituality, and secular commitment, which Vatican II recaptured *almost* faithfully. I say "almost" faithfully, because an old clericalism is yet allowed to appear in the way true worship of the whole church ("spiritual sacrifice") is made subordinate to the ministerial priesthood so as not to give full liturgical value to the priesthood of the faithful—that is, to their *liturgy of life*.

Obviously we have an initial difficulty here, for the word "liturgy" is hardly used in the New Testament in the way Vatican II uses it. Because the Septuagint had restricted the word to mean levitical worship, which was of a ritualistic nature, authentic Christian worship was seldom or never called "liturgy" in the New Testament. The prophets of the Jewish Bible had already insisted that true worship is personal and communal holiness—that is, fidelity to the covenant, obedience to God, and the practice of justice rather than external sacrifices (Jer. 7:21–23, 45ff.; Amos 5:22–24; Isaiah 1:10–20; Hosea 6:6ff.). Jesus, continuing this prophetic tradition, preached an antitemple, antiritual type of worship (John 4:19–26). Fidelity to the new covenant, the gospel of love, becomes the criterion of sanctity.

It was practically for holding this view of spirituality that Jesus was led to death (Matt. 26:61), Stephen martyred (Acts 6:12–14; 7:47–53), and the first persecutions unleashed on the disciples (Acts 8:1). Because the word "liturgy" could not convey this new idea of Christian spirituality, it was avoided by the New Testament writers except for a few instances (Rom. 15:16; Phil. 2:17) and is used only once to designate the collective worship of the Christian assembly (Acts 13:2), for which the normal preference would be *latria* or *douleia*.[1]

"Liturgy" has acquired a new sense in this twentieth century, especially in the Liturgical Constitution of Vatican II. It means the holiness of Christian life constituting the spiritual sacrifice of the self-oblation made to the Father by the whole Body of Christ united in his spirit with him who is its head (liturgy of life), and ecclesially expressed through the sacraments, especially through the eucharist (liturgy as "source and summit"). It comes very close (though not close enough) to the New Testament teaching on Christian worship (more about this below). Let us recall that for St. Paul, baptism was not a mere rite but a (mystical) union with Christ, a dying and rising with him in one's day-to-day life. The eucharist is an act of thanksgiving consisting of a covenantal gesture of breaking, sharing, and pouring out one's life for others. To eat sumptuously while others starved was antieucharistic and antiecclesial, "a sin against the body of the Lord" (see 1 Cor. 11:21, 27). To use three modern concepts retrospectively, this was a (1) *sacramental* (2) *mysticism* of (3) *secular* commitment (in response to the demands of the new covenant of love), the last element being the focal point of the first two. For sacrament and mysticism are intensive moments (the one being ecclesial, the other personal) of the *life of self-sacrifice lived in accordance with the gospel.*

When, unfortunately, sacraments gradually became the remote-control apparatus of a clerical caste (that is, of ministers who "put on" Christ's priesthood without sharing in his victimhood), and therefore the laity abandoned the world of clerics in search of mysticism in the desert (as happened in the fourth century in protest against a church absorbed in the imperialistic worldliness of Rome), the liturgy of the priests and the spirituality of the mystics parted company for good. If uprooted from the day-to-day struggles that the new covenant of love imposes on the Christian conscience (liturgy of life), sacraments and mysticism can never meet. This is why post–Vatican II liberal theology has failed to effect a marriage between them.

Chartres cathedral offers us a sculptor's version of this dichotomy taken for granted in the Middle Ages. Elongated figures of saints thinned out of the world to reach a God above, and the stout, stocky figures of this-worldly artisans and peasants (the worker class from which Jesus came) supporting with the sweat of their brows the leisure class that had the time and energy for liturgies and mystical contemplation, point to a conception of spirituality indelibly sculptured in the cathedrals of our collective unconscious. Only a liberation theology can deliver us from this inversion.

SPIRITUALITY VERSUS SECULAR INVOLVEMENT

Focus on the Theology of the Cross

Further light on this question can come from an inquiry into the second dichotomy: that between *contemplation* and *action*. As in the case of liturgy, here too there is a great deal of confusion arising from a shift of meaning in the words employed. In some early spiritualities *action* meant the mental activity that initiates the psychic processes leading up to the higher realms of *contemplation*. In later terminology, these processes came to be called the ascetical and the mystical "stages" (or more accurately, "aspects") of interior prayer. The former emphasizes the active and the latter points to the passive element in the human search for God, so that both human liberty (as in the first case) and divine gratuity (as in the second case) remain safeguarded.

In current terminology, which has been strongly fostered in recent papal exhortations to priests and religious,[2] action is an apolitical intraecclesial ministry, which, like liturgy in the previous section, is deemed ineffective unless preceded and accompanied by contemplation. Obviously, "action," which should include secular commitments, is more than ecclesiastical apostolates, and the Hellenic notion of "contemplation" implied here tends to compromise the socio-political thrust of the biblical teachings on prayer and worship. Hence, to talk of the present spiritual crisis in terms of this binomial (contemplation and action) is misleading, to say the least. Unfortunately, "prayer" understood as contemplation is often viewed as God-experience, as opposed to "action," which is equated exclusively with human concern.

The use of geometrical concepts, vertical and horizontal, to designate these two aspects, reflects the medieval conception of a God operating from above vertically and of the human person standing in front horizontally! No wonder the aforementioned saints of Chartres cathedral are vertically stretched out and horizontally thin, whereas the poor on whose surplus these saints live are vertically stunted and horizontally overgrown! The contemplatives are "spiritual." The workers and farmers are engrossed in "material" concerns: they are "serfs" who live on the spiritual crumbs that fall from the tables of contemplative "lords." Indeed, a feudal spirituality!

Ignatius of Loyola, who was a *contemplativus simul in actione* (a contemplative in action), elaborated a very significant synthesis that needs to be further broadened and deepened on the strength of his basic intuition into this problem. He subjected both prayer and action to the acid test of authenticity—namely, *self-abnegation*, which is the negative symptom as well as the positive proof of authentic love. All genuine spirituality flows from the spirit of the *crucified* (and exalted) *Christ*. Both contemplation and action can be vitiated by self-seeking, by a veiled refusal to drink of the chalice of Christ or to undergo the baptism of the cross. One recalls here the oft-quoted example of Ignatius's injunction to young Jesuits seeking long hours of prayer—a fashionable trend during his time, as widely indulged in then as oriental mysticism and charismatic movements are in modern times. His demand was that they apply themselves to the duties of their calling in a spirit of self-sacrifice—indeed a reflection of the New Testament teaching on Christian worship as "holy sacrifice" (Rom. 12:1). Once there is self-abnegation, he taught, it would not take long to find God! This precious doctrine, so deeply imbedded in the Western mystical tradition, should be recovered for our times as the authentic criterion of any genuine spirituality.

The christological foundation of this intuition cannot be overstressed— namely, (1) that in the person of *God-Man* Jesus, God and humanity have been so reconciled as to form one indivisible mystery of salvation, and (2) that this reconciliation is effected through the kenosis of the cross, which makes visible and accessible the initial kenosis of the incarnation, and consequently, (3) that the crucified Christ provides, so to say, a link between the divine and the human, so that one can always touch God in humanity, and touch humanity in God, provided one opts for the cross where alone love for God and love for humanity are made convertible. Seek God in total *self-abnegation* and you will touch the depths of the human, your own and that of others. Conversely, commit yourself to human liberation *without any self-seeking*, and you have already experienced God. Without self-abnegation, both prayer and action are delusions, with self-centered introversion parading as interiority, and restless extroversion parading as political commitment.

The accent, therefore, should be on the hard gospel demand for *renunciation*, "denying oneself," the "taking up of the cross," as the *conditio sine qua non* of true discipleship—that is to say, of authentic spirituality. The crisis today is not that there is not enough prayer—something that can never be empirically verified—but that the "modern world," with which Vatican II wants us to dialogue, advocates a fictitious Christ, a Jesus minus his cross, or seeks him where he is not found, or eclipses the real (*unjust*) world where he hangs crucified, calling us to join his struggle.

Let me illustrate this with two biblical models: Abraham's experience of faith in *God* and Moses' struggle for justice for his *people*. These two models demonstrate that a God-ward journey culminates in peoplehood and a people-ward commitment climaxes in God-experience only on the cross where Christ stands reconciling God's *people* with the people's *God*. In Asia these two perspectives explain biblically the two models of "renunciation" advocated by gnostic religions and socialist ideologies, respectively.

In the gospel of John (8:56) Jesus is made to acknowledge that Abraham had met him in history, for "before Abraham ever was, I Am" (John 8:58). Abraham's faith unfolds the agonies of a long search to understand the inner voice in obedience to which he *abandoned* his home and hearth, and launched into the unknown. He was prepared to *renounce* everything, even his one and only son, to that God, who was growing ever greater on Abraham's horizon— even to the point of self-revelation as the God of all humankind. Abraham's detachment supporting his obedience to God is upheld as a paradigm of faith.

Today Christians of all nations and of all times proclaim him their "father-in-faith" wherever the eucharist is celebrated. His God-ward journey culminated in the founding of a people, precisely because he renounced everything in his search and met Jesus in whom God-experience is linked with peoplehood.

Moses, unlike Abraham, started his journey from the other end, from a commitment to "the people," but ended up discovering God, because his journey began with self-negating love. This christological interpretation of the Moses phenomenon is clearly enunciated in the Letter to the Hebrews. He too is singled out, together with Abraham, as one who had a pre-Jesus encounter with Christ, in view, of course, of Jesus of Nazareth, the privileged point of history where the cross of Christ stands until the kingdom of justice and peace is fully installed. Brought up as a nonbeliever, Moses had not yet known Yahweh when he encountered Christ on the cross of heroic renunciation borne in solidarity with the cross of his suffering brethren.

> It was by faith that, when he was grown up, Moses refused to be known as the son of the Pharaoh's daughter, choosing to suffer oppression in the company of God's people rather than enjoy the fleeting pleasures of sin. He considered the insults endured for Christ [the Messiah and the messianic people] greater wealth than the treasures of Egypt [Heb. 11: 24–26].

He refuses to be part of an oppressive system and opts out of it to be with an oppressed people. This option is regarded in the New Testament as an option for Christ, presumably because it was authenticated by the renunciation of his personal security. No wonder his love of others later culminated in a face-to-face encounter with Yahweh on Sinai.

Liberation theology has restored the theology of the cross to the post-Vatican II church. Contemplation and action receive their authenticity not from each other, but from the cross that stands wherever altars are built to mammon on the graves of God's poor. True spirituality, then, is founded on self-transcendence—self-abnegation that grows into self-fulfillment (Matt. 16:25), in and through the *Other*; not only the Other who hides in one's own self waiting to be sought through Prayer, but also this same Other who hides in others as the victim-judge of human injustice (Matt. 25:35–36) waiting to be served through action. Both Abrahamic and Mosaic models of spirituality converge in indicating that Christ can be encountered as God-Man on the cross where God-search and human concern constitute one salvific process—that is to say, one liberational enterprise.

SECULAR INVOLVEMENT VERSUS LITURGY

Focus on Jesus the Man

The contrast between the liberation theology of Latin America and the post-Vatican II theology of the Western patriarchate can be seen also in their respective approaches to the third dichotomy in our list—the one between the secular and the sacramental dimensions of Christian life.

Let us first of all recapture the exact relationship between these two dimensions as advocated in the normative teachings of the New Testament. Instead of quoting any Latin American theologian, I will cite one of Europe's foremost spokesmen of post–Vatican II progressive theology, Edward Schillebeeckx.[3] In an inimitably concise summary of the New Testament doctrine on "secular life as worship," he analyzes the notion of liturgy within the purview of Jesus the man: "Jesus did not give his life in a liturgical solemnity. . . . On the contrary, in an obvious secular conflict, colored though it was by religion, he remained faithful to God and to men [sic] and gave his life for his own in a secular combination of circumstances." Therefore, "Calvary was not a Church liturgy, but an *hour of human life* which Jesus *experienced as worship*. In it our redemption is to be found."

According to the interpretation given in the Letter to the Hebrews, Schillebeeckx thinks that "it is possible to speak of a secular liturgy." Cult, he argues, has acquired a new meaning in the New Testament, and a new concept of worship is offered us: "Human life itself experienced as liturgy or as worship of God." For "on the basis of Jesus' self-sacrifice, the Christian's life in this world can now become worship." Thus "the New Testament clearly lays stress on secular worship." Then he concludes that "Christian commitment to the ordering of human society here and now and the Christian opposition to all injustices that disrupt peace" among human beings are not only scripturally justifiable but are to be "experienced as that secular worship required by the biblical essence of Christianity," wherefore "Christian faith is not a flight from the world to the church's liturgy."

Schillebeeckx here seems to use the word "liturgy" in the Vatican II sense—namely, both as "secular liturgy" (that is, his own term for secular commitments lived *as* worship) and as "church's liturgy" or "liturgical solemnity" (his terms for the sacramental expression of the secular liturgy, especially the eucharistic celebration). Then he raises the question that engages our attention here: Is Christianity merely an "intensified human solidarity" (obviously he is referring to the secular liturgy) or is it also a "song of praise" and a "festal gathering" (church liturgy, especially eucharistic celebration)?

For conciliar theology the answer seems clear: church liturgy is the "source and summit" (*fons et culmen*) of the liturgy of life. The Christian commitment—that is, living the gospel in a spirit of self-sacrifice, as *sequela Christi* (following of Christ)—both originates and culminates in the official liturgical gathering of God's people celebrating redemption sacramentally (especially in that song of praise called the eucharist wherein the church offers itself "through him, with him, and in him" in the oneness of the Spirit as an act of praise to the Father).

This emphasis on church liturgy as "source and summit" is understandable if seen as part of a perspective that germinated in the monastico-clerical ethos of pre–Vatican II liturgical renewal. First of all a subtle overemphasis on the hierarchical role in the liturgy seems to weaken somewhat the baptismal basis of liturgy, so that "secular liturgy" (to use Schillebeeckx's terminology) has to *participate* in the liturgy that seems to preexist in the hierarchically constituted church (that is, in the church liturgy). Secondly, it looks as if the church, as God's people continuing the mystery of Jesus' humanity by being the locus and subject of Christian worship, is made subordinate to the symbolic presence of Christ in the institutional church and in the institutional liturgy. Here, in the words of the council, we hear the voice of Odo Casel and perhaps also de la Taille.

How would all this appear in the context of a life-and-death struggle for justice, where "festal gathering" and "song of praise" constitute privileged moments of strength and joy, a profound contemplation and joyous celebration of the mysteries revealed in the humanity of Jesus, as is known from the Gospels as well as through one's own personal encounters with Jesus? In such a perspective (that is to say, if liberationist logic is to be adhered to with rigorous consistency), we presume that the liturgy of the official church would originate and culminate in the *liturgy of life*, which is the primary guarantee of salvation/sanctification, and not the other way around!

This logic is based on the primacy that a liberation theology would accord to the humanity of the historical Jesus, and the subordination of the church to it. The adage, *ubi ecclesia ibi Christus* (where the church is, there is Christ) is not only reversed to *ubi Christus ibi ecclesia*, but this Christ, in whose company the authentic church is found, is clearly perceived as the incarnate Christ of history continuing his presence "sacramentally" in the flesh and blood of human beings (his least brethren) crying, if not also striving, for the dawn of the kingdom of justice, and not primarily in a gnostic Christ legitimizingly present in an institutionalized community with an institutionalized worship.

The ministerial church is, of course, invited to offer the *occasion* to transubstantiate this human flesh and blood, broken and shared in the struggle for true peace, that this flesh and blood may become the "celebration of the eucharist"—Jesus' own song of thanksgiving and hope. If the structure of the church renders it utterly incapable of offering this *occasion*—which is what I mean by "church liturgy"—then it could be that it is already cut off from its head, the Christ. It would cease to be the church, and much less would it be the locus of the *fons et culmen* of secular worship! True perception of Jesus in his historical human dimension leads to a search for the true liturgy of the authentic church. The ministerial church, by becoming *ecclesiolae* or "basic communities" where Christ enacts his paschal mystery in spirit and in flesh, "learns" to be the authentic bearer of Christ's presence (*ecclesia discens*) (the learning church) and thus retrieves its lost authority (*ecclesia docens*) (the teaching church). This is the "ecclesiological revolution" that liberation theology generates by subordinating church liturgy to the liturgy of life. It was Jesus' style of building the church through Calvary, through that hour of human life that he experienced as worship.

To bring out in bold relief the novelty and the challenge of liberation theology in this regard, one would do well to recall the manner in which the humanity of Christ is reaffirmed from time to time within the nonliberational perspectives of classic theologies. The humanity of Christ is eclipsed in theology wherever the human element is neglected in spirituality. Then there arise waves of secular humanism, which percolate into the conscious center of the church in the form of a "cult of humanity" in the supreme sense of the term— that is, a cult of Jesus, the most human God and the most divine human being. Every search for liberated humanity coincides with the innate thirst for the "God-Human" Christ. Every humanism, when "christianized," is immediately transfigured into a "Jesus movement."

In the late medieval period nonhumanistic tendencies were registered in a theology that filtered God through scholastic abstractions, disincarnate spiritualities that reduced the God-human encounter to a mystical merging of a human soul (minus the body) with the divine Spirit (minus Christ's humanity), and in a juridicism that diminished human persons to mere papal "subjects." Along with those tendencies, there was also a surging of *popular devotions to the humanity of Christ*, restoring sanity within the church. The devotions to *Corpus Christi*, the Precious Blood, the Five Wounds, and the like, were a liturgical reeducation of the church in the basics of Christianity. Franciscan devotions to the crib and the cross still keep us firm on essentials.

The devotion to the Sacred Heart, which has its remote origins in the writings of Saints Gertrude and Mechtilde, is certainly the most widespread and, theologically, the most elaborated cult of Jesus' humanity. It became situated in the bosom of the church when the Jesuits gave it special articulation in theory and praxis, and thus compensated for the lack of Christocentric devotions in the clerical liturgies of the time, which were far removed from the people. The magisterium listened to the theologians and made the devotion its own and even issued an encyclical on it. If the devotion has lost its relevance today, it is because the liturgy, now renewed, makes it redundant.

My hope is that a similar process will take place in the church from the new emphasis on the humanity of Christ that comes from the praxis of the basic communities. May the magisterium make it its own. Let me immediately say why.

A theology that is nonliberational could produce "devotions," but a liberation theology stimulates commitments to Jesus who is God-become-our-neighbor. It is a shift from the Christ of contemplation to the Christ with flesh and blood. Strange as it may sound, the classic devotion to the Sacred Heart revolved so much around the theory of "reparation" for the damage done to that heart, that it could easily lead followers to a pathological inversion unless they really found that there existed in reality a Christ capable of suffering damage and, therefore, reparable. Liberation theology puts us in touch with such a Christ, whose bleeding heart demands brave deeds of love, a Christ hungry, thirsty, naked, sick, homeless, and fettered by social chains (Matt. 25:31–46), Christ the laborer's son (Matt. 13:55), Christ without a place to be born (Luke 2:7), to lay his head (Matt. 8:20) or to be buried (Matt. 27:60), Christ who was a threat to Herod's security and, therefore, hunted down by him (Matt. 2:13), Christ calumniated before the court of law (Luke 23:1–8),

Christ in chains in the praetorium (Mark 15:16), Christ tortured by the army (Matt. 27:26), Christ a criminal among criminals (Luke 23:39), Christ the victim of priestly fanaticism and political opportunism (Matt. 27:11–23), Christ the unwanted leader (John 19:14–15).

This human Christ corresponds to the Christian humanism of our times, which enlightens us about the hidden roots of dehumanization, proposes an alternative model of society where human growth rather than profit-accumulation (mammon) is the motivating force, and spells out a process of discernment not different from the classical method: identification of the enemy, choice of strategy, and struggle for the kingdom with confidence and hope in divine grace. The Christ who emerges from this humanism is not merely a Good Friday Christ, who would inspire us only to a pathological messianism in social questions, with no room for humor, esthetic experience, and person-to-person intimacy—all ingredients of genuine human growth. Rather, it is a figure of Christ brightened in the light of the resurrection, a Christ who calls dust to life, a Christ who heals, a Christ who feeds the multitude, a Christ who removes social stigmas (leprosy) and reintegrates outcasts into society—in short, Christ the restorer of all things, who suffers pain but struggles in hope, a Christ exalted even on the cross.

Would that the theologians who articulate this devotion to the humanity of Christ and participate in his paschal mystery in the liturgy of life be heard with sympathy by the official church, which paid respect to mere devotions of the past!

2

To Be Poor as Jesus Was Poor?

The Ecumenical Association of Third World Theologians (EATWOT) has made repeated appeals to the universal church to focus its attention on the plight of the poor as the pole of reference in its theology, and to make the poor both the point of departure and the point of arrival of its spirituality inasmuch as God's concern for the poor is the axial theme of the Bible as a whole.[1] The EATWOT thesis on spirituality can be contracted into a three-point formula: a Christian is a person who has made an irrevocable option *to follow* Jesus; this option necessarily coincides with the option *to be poor*; but the "option to be poor" becomes a true "following of Jesus" only to the extent that it is also an option *for the poor*. Christian discipleship or "spirituality," therefore, is a coincidence of all these three options.

The (theo)logical force of this argument is derived from two biblical axioms: the irreconcilable antagonism between God and wealth, and the irrevocable covenant between God and the poor, Jesus himself being this covenant. These two principles imply that, in Jesus, God and the poor have formed an alliance against their common enemy: mammon. This is what justifies the conclusion that, for both Jesus and his followers, spirituality is not merely a *struggle to be poor* but equally a *struggle for the poor*.

SPIRITUALITY AS A STRUGGLE TO BE POOR

The irreconcilable antinomy between God and money (Matt. 6:24), or more precisely between *Abba* and *Mamona* (to use two emotionally loaded and, to that extent, untranslatable Aramaic words that the synoptics place exclusively on the lips of Jesus), is the vital nucleus of the gospel message as expanded in the Sermon on the Mount. Growing intimacy with the one and constant repudiation of the other characterize the whole mission of Jesus on earth. He is our covenant with God. Whoever has a pact with mammon is excluded from fellowship with his Father, "for no one can serve two masters." The rich young man is asked to become poor before becoming his disciple (Matt. 19:21).

The kingdom Jesus preached—that is, the salvation he offered—is not meant for the rich (Luke 6:20, 24)—or at least it is too difficult for them unless God's miraculous intervention helps them renounce their possessions and enter the kingdom (Matt. 19:23–26). If this was Jesus' conviction, is it surprising that

---

First published in *The Way*, 24 (1984) 186-97 whose editor had requested the author to deal with the question of poverty in the context of the second week of the Spiritual Exercises of St. Ignatius.

he resorted to physical violence at the mere sight of money polluting the religion of his day (John 2:13-17)?

In Christian ascetical literature, both exterior renunciation of goods and interior resignation to God are normally conveyed by the word "poverty." St. Ignatius of Loyola seems to have epitomized the whole spirituality of Jesus in that single word. In his vocabulary, the surrender of one's wealth to the poor and the surrender of one's will to God appear as "actual poverty" and "spiritual poverty," respectively (*Exercises,* 98, 146, 147). If taken in the dynamic sense of a spiritual struggle, rather than in the Hellenistic sense of a static virtue, "poverty" is by far the most comprehensive term to describe the ethos of the "Jesus event." It recaptures for us Christ's own attitudes, options, and pattern of behavior, all of which together make up the human texture of his redemptive mission on earth. To understand this is to know him; to practice this is to follow him.

Poverty, however, is not merely a material rejection of wealth, because mammon is more than just money. It is a subtle force operating within me, an acquisitive instinct driving me to be the rich fool whom Jesus ridicules in the parable of the harvester who wanted to tear down his grain bins and build larger ones (Luke 12:13-21). Or again, mammon is what I do with money and what it does to me; what it both promises and brings when I come to terms with it: security and success, power and prestige—acquisitions that make me appear privileged. It makes me seem to possess a special gift for leadership. I may even experience an irresistible satisfaction in being revered and sought after as a guide and guru, or being chosen to exert great influence over others—of course, for the glory of God and the salvation of souls.

It was precisely this model of leadership that occasioned a crisis in Jesus' faith in the Father, especially when he became conscious of God's power surging from deep within him; when his touch began to heal, his words vibrated with authority, and the tumultuous crowds flocked to him. Was he not *the* teacher of Israel, *the* leader of the people, *the* prophet of God, and, who knows, the long awaited Messiah?

Furthermore, the image of the charismatic leader had been distorted beyond recognition by many pretenders who, according to Flavius Josephus, claimed that God would vindicate their messianic election by working prodigies in the presence of their enemies, as God did when Moses spoke to the pharaoh. There was also a current of popular enthusiasm that readily welcomed this exhibitionist kind of "prophetic" ministry.

Note, therefore, that when tempted by the Pharisees and the Sadducees to produce a sign from above to prove his divine election, Jesus spurned the suggestion, calling the tempters "an evil and adulterous generation" and insinuating, by an allusion to Jonah, that his authority would be vindicated only after he had been thoroughly humiliated before his enemies (Matt. 16:1-4)! By that time, Jesus had passed through what is called the "Galilean crisis"; his popularity waning and his loneliness deepening, he had come to realize that "he has failed in his mission as he had previously understood it" and had successfully overcome the opposite temptation to withdraw into himself by way of overreaction.[2]

He has now abandoned all hope of seeing immediate success in his mission. Unless he himself dies as a victim of the prevailing mammonic order, there is no way for God's new order to dawn. And so he begins to speak of the cross openly, not only as his personal destiny but as the only path open to those who ✓ dare to walk with him to the kingdom. The new humanity will not be achieved by power and prestige, but by weakness, failure, and humiliation. The image of the popular leader of Israel yields place to that of the suffering servant of Yahweh. "What is thought of highly by humans is loathsome in the sight of God," he reminds the Pharisees, "who loved money" and "laughed at him" for what he taught about God and mammon (Luke 16:13–15).

This new vision needed to be reaffirmed and this option had to be renewed ✓ several times during his life (Matt. 20:20–28; Mark 8:31–33; Luke 9:51–54; John 6:15; 18:36) and particularly during the last decisive hours of his earthly mission (Mark 14:32; Matt. 26:52–53) when he had to resurrender his will to *Abba*, his Father. For he strove to steer clear of even the semblance of pseudo messianism.[3]

Hence the question: Could one really fathom the quality and the intensity of Jesus' allegiance to the Father except by monitoring his recurrent conflicts with mammon—that is to say, his many "temptations" that he himself was not ashamed to speak about (Luke 22:28)? His poverty was indeed a painful growth in grace and wisdom through a process of unending discernment of God's will in the face of these many temptations, which some theologians ✓ would not hesitate to call "crises of self-identity,"[4] crises provoked by new demands from the Father and the changing tactics of mammon.

Poverty, then, was Jesus' characteristic posture toward God and mammon, ◡ which, however, his closest associates could not comprehend even after the resurrection until they received the Spirit (Acts 1:6–8). For only a divine initiative could make them "know the Son" (Matt. 11:27). Once his Spirit was given to them—that is, when they acquired a connaturality with the spirit of the Master—they were not slow to recognize the conflicts that shaped Jesus' spirituality. By means of a clever literary device, the evangelists presented this lifelong struggle against mammon in the form of a three-act drama with the ◡ desert as the stage and his messianic investiture at the Jordan as the immediate contextual background (Matt. 4:1–11 and parallels). This pericope on "Jesus' triple temptation in the desert" was meant not only to recall, by contrast, the temptations that overpowered the first messianic people in the desert when it lost confidence in Yahweh and preferred to make a god of gold, but also to educate the new messianic people—the nascent church—in the ways of the Master as it too was now beginning to meet the very same temptations that its founder once faced.

What is strange, then, if the church too is continually led by the Spirit into the desert to be tempted? Poverty after all is a spirituality of struggle. There is never a dearth of crises, so long as mammon is a power to reckon with. But each new temptation brings with it a new motive and a new way "to be poor as Jesus was poor."

When, for instance, very early in its history, the church changed from a powerless people to an influential force in imperial Rome, the exodus of Christians to the desert in search of the true spirit of Christ challenged its triumphalism and threw it into a crisis of identity that men like Basil and Benedict partially resolved by bringing the desert experience from the periphery of the church to its center, so that the monk came to be a symbol of Christian poverty.

Similarly when Western medieval society was being disoriented by incipient mercantile economics and growing urbanization, the Waldensians initiated a centrifugal force within the church through their justifiable quest for "the indigent Jesus" outside ecclesiastical structures, a quest that received a centripetal impetus in the Franciscan movement. In these mendicants, the church recovered for itself and for society in general a new framework for Christian poverty.

When Ignatius Loyola stepped into the ecclesiastical world, Paul III had already appointed a reform commission, in 1536. Its agenda, contrary to expectation, showed no preoccupation with schisms, heresies, or lapses in celibacy, which were at most symptoms, not the disease. The real malaise, according to its diagnosis, was the abuse of wealth in the church, nepotism, and simony, and the existence of an "ecclesiastical rabble" accounted for by the prevalence of a parallel class of wealth-accumulating clerics. The Ignatian *Exercises* are not without allusions to these problems. What Ignatius offered the church was not "reform," and much less "counterreform" (a task left to the Council of Trent), but a "renewal" from below. He summoned the rank and file of the church to anchor themselves in Jesus' own spirituality, at least in spiritual poverty if not also in material poverty.

Unfortunately, the theology he had learned did not help him to see that poverty (both material and spiritual) was meant to be the basic spirituality of *all* Christians and not an "evangelical counsel" like celibacy, which is a charism given to the few; and that even in the case of ordained ministers, the policy of "obligatory celibacy and optional poverty" was the exact converse of what Jesus had intended. Nonetheless, Ignatius would have unhesitatingly concurred with Theo Van Asten's famous intervention at the Synod of 1971:

> Why does the church demand that priests renounce founding a family and not demand *also* that they renounce honors and titles, even ecclesiastical ones, as well as the pursuit of worldly goods? There is, after all, a scale of values in the Gospels to be respected.[5]

In the Gospels, God's competitor is not sex or marriage but mammon. Hence it is poverty, not primarily celibacy, that guarantees one's "undivided devotion to God." Both celibacy and sex can lose their relativity and sacramentality, and thus degenerate into objects of an idolatrous cult. Both can be vitiated by mammon.

Even in Indian cultures where the renunciation of marriage is a supreme sign of sanctity, celibates are not reckoned persons of God if they are also persons of means. Gandhi, on the other hand, four times a father, was virtually "canonized" by the Indian masses for having renounced all material goods and comforts for God and the people. The masses were illiterate and could not have read his admission that, after their fourth child, he and his wife vowed sexual continence. But even the few who read it had no difficulty in believing him. What rendered him credible were his other visible forms of renunciation—his "material poverty." For chastity can never be seen without its fruits, which it can never produce unless it is cross-fertilized with poverty. Celibacy minus poverty is comfortable bachelorhood or convenient spinsterhood! Was this not also St. Ambrose's grouse against vestal virgins?[6]

Ignatius never confused mammon with its shadow. He fought no futile wars against an imaginary enemy of God (such as "matter" or "the world," "marriage" or "the woman") as did the Encratites before him or the Jansenists after him [these latter were reputed to have been as pure as angels and as proud as devils]. At the most decisive moment in his *Spiritual Exercises*, Ignatius confronts the would-be follower of Christ with two irreconcilable alternatives (or "standards" as he calls them): either riches, the anti-God, which demolishes the kingdom through the *pride* that issues from vainglory; or poverty, the antimammon that builds up the kingdom through *humility*, the fruit of humiliations (*Exercises*, 135–47). That "big is ugly and small is beautiful" is neatly contrasted in his graphic description of Lucifer in Babylon promoting the first alternative and Jesus in Jerusalem pleading for the second. These were the policies at work in the church and the society of his day. They were also the two models of messianic leadership that confronted Jesus in subtle guises throughout the entire desert of his life and death.

At this point, in view of what I intend to discuss in the second part of this chapter, some lessons can be drawn from what has been said so far. Note first that Ignatius, neither a theologian nor an exegete, nevertheless acquired an accurate grasp of Jesus' spirituality, which modern exegesis confirms almost to the letter.[7] The secret lies in his *method*. In his contemplation he tried to *know* Jesus in order to follow him, and in his poverty he *followed* him in order to know him.

Secondly, Ignatius preserved for us the ancient view of spirituality as poverty, and poverty as *struggle*, without falling into a Manichean dualism, for, even in his mythological framework of demonism, the concrete choice is between riches and poverty, and even then victory is ensured for those who make the second option. Ignatius also refined the idea of struggle in his "Rules for Discernment," in which the subtle maneuvers of "the enemy of human nature" as they occur in the finer areas of the human spirit are exposed with an introspective acumen unsurpassed in the history of Christian spirituality. But these rules cover only the battlefields within the intrahuman sphere. At the interhuman level, we have all succumbed to the enemy. Mammon, whom some (Western, not Latin American) theologians have aptly nicknamed Capital,[8] interferes with God's kingdom not merely as a psychological drive but as a gigantic sociological force alienating us not only from God but from one another in and through a social order that can thrive only on the coexistence of waste and want. New skills are required to discern how to decrease the wastefulness of the affluent (struggle to be poor) and how to eliminate want (struggle for the poor).

SPIRITUALITY AS A STRUGGLE FOR THE POOR

Any discourse on 'poverty' can be confusing if the polysemous nature of the word is not respected. Leonardo Boff assigns at least five meanings to it.[9] I submit that in the final analysis there are only two basic concepts to be distinguished: *voluntary poverty,* which I have been discussing so far, and *forced poverty*, which engages my attention here. The first is the seed of liberation; the second is the fruit of sin. The kingdom of God can be viewed in terms of a universal practice of the one and *consequent* elimination of the other.

I emphasize *consequent*. The rich man in search of eternal life—that is, in search of God—is asked to give up mammon in such a way that the poor would benefit by his renunciation (Mark 10:21). Voluntary poverty is an indispensable prerequisite for the just order of society wherein forced poverty has no right to exist: such was the kingdom Jesus preached. In fact his precursor, in preparing the people for his coming, invited them to share their *extra* clothes and food with those having none (Luke 3:11). If, indeed, Lazarus remained hungry till his death, was it not because of a rich man's wastefulness: his refusal to share even his *excess* goods, "the crumbs falling from the table" (Luke 16:19–31)? Poverty thus forced upon a brother or a sister is an evil, the removal of which is a burden Jesus laid at the door of the rich. In other words, the affluent are called to be poor so that there be no poor.

Wealth, therefore, is an evil only when accumulated. Bread too is a "sin against the body of the Lord" if consumed by a few while others starve (see 1 Cor. 11:21, 27). But when broken and shared, it is *his* body that we consume and become. If wealth, too, is distributed "according to need" so "that there be no needy person" (see Acts 4:34–35), it ceases to be mammon. It becomes sacramental. Hence the seemingly outrageous doctrine of the church fathers (Chrysostom, Jerome, Ambrose, Augustine): if some are poor, it is because some others have acquired or inherited "more," and this "more" remains stolen property until it is shared with the poor.[10] If this is so, then Boff's observation, "poverty can be cured by poverty,"[11] has deep roots in Christian tradition.

I am glad that this message is also the "secular gospel" preached by the ILO

International Institute for Social Studies in Geneva. Its director, Albert Tevoedjre, in a curiously titled book, *Poverty: Wealth of Peoples*[12] (evidently a rejoinder to Adam Smith's classic), defines poverty as the "state of someone who has what is necessary and not the surplus." He suggests that only such poverty can eradicate present inequalities, provided of course that the poor nations form a solidarity contract in view of this struggle.

Economics apart, there is also a *christological* basis for this doctrine. I am not referring to a sociological dream or a purely ethical principle, but a specifically Christian spirituality that requires of us a leap of faith.

There is, in other words, a "christic factor" by which "poverty" (giving up the "more") is intrinsically oriented toward the liberation of the poor. For God in God's very self, having *opted* to be *born* in Jesus the Son (2 Cor. 8:9; Phil. 2:6-8), has gathered as God's body a new people comprising these two categories of the poor: the poor by "option" who are the *followers of Jesus* (Matt. 19:21), and the poor by "birth" who are the *proxies of Christ* (Matt. 25:31-46). In other words, the struggle to be poor cannot be a recognizably Christian spirituality if it is not inspired by each of these motives: to *follow Jesus* who *was* poor then, and to *serve Christ* who *is* in the poor now. One clear implication of this "christic factor" is this: the few who renounce their possessions are not "founded and rooted in Christ Jesus" if the many who have no possessions to renounce are not the beneficiaries of that renunciation. This again is an interpretation of evangelical poverty with ancient roots and conserved for us by a line of saints who vigorously resisted all temptations to the contrary.

The anchorite tradition, as exemplified in the *Vita Antonii* and based on the call narratives (esp. Matt. 19:21), never advocated any renunciation of wealth that was not made in favor of the poor. It was the Pachomian *cenobia* that introduced the dangerous custom of allowing candidates to donate their belongings to the community they were joining. Not only did the poor not benefit by their renunciation, but the "renouncers" came to be cushioned by an institutional security. Even manual labor, initially introduced to ensure a poor lifestyle, soon ended up with an accumulation of a surplus, thus defeating the very purpose of such experiments. St. Basil's remedy was the small community earning its bare needs, for, as he rightly held, what is owned by those dedicated to God belongs to God and *therefore* it must be given to the poor.[13]

Here the oft-quoted Jerusalem experiment (Acts 4:32-37) could be as misleading as it is inspiring. No doubt it was a symbolic effort—like so many others that followed it in subsequent centuries. Even if that experiment had failed, we still say, it was an experiment worth failing. Small efforts at creating "sacraments of the kingdom" wherein "no one claimed for one's own use anything that one had, for everything they owned was held in common" (see Acts 4:32) must recur in history countless times before a dent can be made in human consciousness.

But this experiment by no means justifies a collective ownership of wealth limited to the members of the community and not including the rights of the needy outside that community in its policy of sharing. The appeal to individual and spiritual poverty at the expense of collective and material poverty is a futile attempt to follow Jesus the poor man without ministering to Christ in the poor. Francis of Assisi, who held these two ideals together, "changed the vow of sharing goods to a vow of poverty which was binding on the whole group and not merely on the individual."[14]

This is in fact the Ignatian method I alluded to in the first part of this chapter. It is the dialectics of knowing Christ and following Jesus in and through the practice of poverty.

This is also the "hermeneutical circle" between theory and praxis that animates the numerous grassroot communes that spring up on the fringes of the church especially in the Third World. There is, however, one difference that sets them apart from traditional religious communities in the church. As paradigms of the future, these communities project an image of chosen poverty that stretches far beyond the symbolic level of their own experiment to the level of international justice. Perceiving mammon to be much more than inordinate affections, which are to be detected only by introspective discernment, they regard the colossal scandal of poverty as the fruit of institutionalized greed. Ignatius himself, in his meditation on the "Two Standards," did not fail to point out the seductive manner in which the mammonic system is advertised in "all the world not omitting any provinces, places, states, nor any persons in particular" (*Exercises*, 141)—and, I might add, all institutions, religious and secular. This was the question that brought monks from East and West together at the Benedictine Centenary Congress in Kandy in 1980 and their verdict was unanimous. Though it is primarily in contemplative prayer that the cry of the poor is heard, there exists the "need to undertake serious, even scientific analysis of the causes of poverty and of the various mechanisms which produce it." This is because "poverty is the fruit of sinfulness, oppressive social structures, of corruption in certain countries, and of an unjust international economic order."[15]

Self-analysis alone is therefore inadequate to discern the contemporary strategies of mammon; social analysis must complement it. This is a contention difficult to refute when history records so many instances of individual ascetics living complacently in a socially sinful situation. Buddhists provide us with an example that has many parallels in Christian history. Mongolian lamaseries practiced a common ownership of enormous tracts of land. Despite their disciplined life within their cells, they did not perceive the incongruity of their economic power until the Marxists, as it were, forced them to practice "voluntary" poverty in order to alleviate the *real* poverty of Mongolian peasants!

This is not the only instance in history when a religious group, bound by a vow of poverty, had to wait for a violent turn of events to begin practicing what common sense and their own religious instinct had always enjoined on them. One reason is that a *sociological perception* of poverty—be it poverty voluntarily embraced or poverty structurally imposed—has not been sufficiently assimilated into the religious traditions of humankind, not to speak of the church's own traditional understanding of "spirituality."

This is not to say that the magisterium has not made any attempt to integrate the "struggle to be poor" with the "struggle for the poor." In his *Evangelica Testificatio*, Paul VI moved in this direction when he declared that evangelical poverty carried with it the obligation to awaken human consciences to the demands of social justice by a commitment to and solidarity with [the struggle of] the poor (no. 18) and also the obligation to call upon the rich to act responsibly toward the needy (no. 20).[16]

Whoever defines spirituality as a search for God (and I agree) must not lose sight of the two biblical axioms mentioned at the beginning of this chapter. If the God-mammon antinomy is perceived within God's covenant with the poor—that is, within God's partiality to the oppressed who (according to the Rules for Discernment of Sinful Structures) are the waste product of this earth's wealth-accumulating plutocracy—then a neutral God would be unjust and would violate God's own covenant. Rather, we have a God who assumes the struggle *of* the poor as God's own so that it becomes the divine struggle *for* the poor, the struggle God launched against the proud, the powerful, and the rich (Luke 1:51-53). We *become one with God* (is this not the aim of all mysticism?) to the degree that our poverty drives us to appropriate God's concern for the poor as our own mission.

Here, too, let Jesus' temptations be our guide. Let us purge our minds of the exhibitionist model of social messianism whereby we become heroes of altruism at the expense of the poor. Far from being the subjects of their own emancipation, they remain perpetual objects of our compassion thanks to our organized charity, or instruments of our self-aggrandizement thanks to our "organized struggles." Here a symbiosis of psychological and sociological approaches to discernment is imperative. An introspective analysis should make us question the honesty of our social involvement in the light of a social analysis of the structures that so easily allow us to exploit the poor for our personal fulfillment. The source of this exploitation once again could be the monies that flow in "for the poor"!

Whoever dares to be with God on the side of the poor must renounce all hope of being a hero. It is the criminal's fate—the cross—that Jesus holds out as the banner under which victory is assured. The disciple is not greater than the master. If the master is the victim-judge of oppression (Matt. 25:31-46), disciples too must become victims of the present order or else they have no right to denounce it. The struggle for the poor is a mission entrusted only to those who are or have become poor.

3

Ideology and Religion:
Some Debatable Points

PROBLEMS OF DEFINITION

In all organized activities of religiously committed persons there is invariably an ideology at work. In Christianity, for instance, there is no theology that is ideologically free. "Let him who has no ideology cast the first stone!" This was a pebble that one Latin American bishop tossed back at some of his colleagues when they charged that liberation theologians were ideologically biased. We can never point at somebody else's ideological blinkers except by seeing them through our own. The question, then, is not whether ideology is compatible with religion but "which ideology is compatible with which kind of religion?"

What, then, is ideology? There is no consensus as to a definition. But the disagreement is not as wide as in the case of "religion," which, according to Schebasta, has over one hundred fifty definitions circulating in Western universities today. Collating its essential features as they occur in various definitions, I can construe my own notion of ideology without implying that all the features I list here are accepted by all:

(a) a worldview,
(b) essentially programmatic,
(c) about a this-worldly future to be realized, not without a struggle, in the socio-political order,
(d) with the aid of certain tools of analysis or a method of discernment based on its own (that is, ideological) premises,
(e) and requiring by its own intrinsic nature to be transcended by the truth it seeks to articulate.

This no doubt is a compact formula and needs to be spelled out. The best way to begin doing so would be to compare this notion of ideology with the two cognate concepts of religion and philosophy.

Philosophy in its modern Western sense is no more than a coherent worldview meant only to *explain* the world. "The point, however, is to *change* it," said Marx. Ideology, on the other hand, is a programmatic worldview. Besides

First published in the Sri Lanka journal *Dialogue,* 10 (1983) 31-41 as part of a double issue dealing with the theme "Reflections on the Buddhist-Christian Dialogue on Occasion of the One-Hundredth Anniversary of the Death of Karl Marx."

being a "vision" of a future envisaged as an improvement on the present, it also includes a "mission" to change present disorder in accordance with that future. There is, here, a sense of "evangelical" urgency that is totally alien to philosophy.

The Oriental notion of philosophy, in some points at least, coincides with that of ideology, for in the East, unlike in the West, philosophy and religion are not split apart. Philosophy in the Orient is a religious vision and religion is a philosophy of life. An Asian philosophy is not only a worldview (*darsana*) but is equally a program of action (*pratipada*). Thus, for instance, in Buddhist soteriology, the salvific truth (*satya*) is not conceived of apart from the salvific path (*marga*), and vice versa.

Nevertheless, religion (whether it overlaps with philosophy as in the East, or stands apart from it as in the West) differs radically from ideology in one significant point: its concept of the future. From this difference flow all others.

Religion, *primarily* and *normatively* (but not exclusively), points to an Absolute Future, a Totally Other, so that the horizon of final liberation is given a metacosmic ultimacy, if not also a *lokottara* distance. But, contrary to a widespread misconception, religion does emphatically teach that the Absolute Future has to be anticipated here in this life not only through the spiritual achievements of individual persons but also through visible structures in human society. Thus in Buddhism a distinction is made between the final liberation that comes after death (*parammarana nirvāna*) and its anticipation on earth (*dittha-dhamma nirvāna*). Moreover, at the social level, we have the *savakasangha*, which is meant to be a visible communion of ungreedy men and women, constituting the paradigm of a liberated society. Christianity makes the same point by its teachings on the "eschatological tension" between the *not-yet* and the *already* of the kingdom of God. Christians are called to live out the Beatitudes (Sermon on the Mount) here on earth in order to form a Christian community that is an ecclesial anticipation of the final communion.

Ideology, on the other hand, precludes from its programmatic worldview even the semblance of a metacosmic future. It is *exclusively* concerned with what it conceives to be a radical amelioration of the socio-political order with concomitant changes in the psycho-spiritual sphere. Its target is a this-worldly secular progress that may or may not be compatible with the metacosmic goal that a given religion speaks of. It is usually the case that a religion, in incarnating the Absolute Future here on earth, makes use of visible social structures, strategies, and institutions that (this-worldly) ideologies provide.

Historical Background

That religion has always been mixed up with ideology is a hindsight of some contemporary thinkers, for the whole concept of ideology was first articulated only a few centuries ago. A word about this history, therefore, might throw further light on the peculiar interrelationship between religion and ideology.

The word "ideology" entered our vocabulary thanks to the French philosopher Destutt de Tracy, who employed it for the first time in the simple literal sense of "a science of ideas"—not any science, of course, but one that is put at the service of humanity. Quite significantly, this concept was born at the time of the French Revolution, which saw the power of three ideas—equality, fraternity, and liberty—creating far-reaching changes in human history.

It is equally significant that this revolution had as its avowed enemy and as the target of its attacks the inhuman political leadership and the insensitive religious hierarchy of the day. The protagonists of religion (the higher clergy, propertied and acting in collusion with the ruling nobility) pointed with one hand to the remote metacosmic goal of "eternal happiness in heaven," while, with the other hand, they pampered themselves with God's earthly blessings denied to the masses. The growing dissatisfaction with religion—that is, the increasing disillusion about its capacity to bring about immediate relief to the suffering masses—was quite in evidence in the French Revolution.

There was, thus, an unconscious search for a secular counterpart of religion that would concern itself with a this-worldly future to which a passionate commitment was called for. It could be said now, retrospectively, that the object of this search was what some of us today would describe as "ideology"; not, of course, an ideology that justified the privileges of the dominant class, but one that fostered equality and freedom for all.

The subsequent growth of secularization, or dereligionization, of politics, as well as the proliferation of antireligious humanisms in the very next century— the nineteenth—was accompanied by the emergence of many such "ideologies," though at that time they were not designated by that name. The appalling failure of religious leaders to assess the nature of, and procure remedies for, the evils that accompanied the Industrial Revolution allowed such "ideological" pursuits to end up being not merely secular or nonreligious but also positively antireligious. Marxism was the most articulate ideology of that kind and Marxists themselves recognize it by that name.

Ideology in the Pejorative Sense

Would Marx have agreed to such an appellation? Or was Marx too much concerned with detecting oppressive kinds of ideology to have acknowledged his own to be a "liberative" species of the same genus? His well-known definition of ideology as the *corruption of reason by interest* indicates that he directed his efforts at analyzing what he (borrowing a Hegelian phrase) would describe as a false consciousness of both the victims and creators of an unjust social order—that is, the unconscious rationalization by which both parties accept a particular social order as necessary because it is allegedly ordained by God, or destined by nature, or sanctified by tradition, or sanctioned by religion. Hence, what Marx first detected as operative in society was *ideology in the pejorative sense of the term*: a rational justification of the status quo, or the unexamined theory behind an immoral praxis.

Sigmund Freud, who came later, discovered for us the subtle manner in which reason gets corrupted by interest deep down at the level of the uncon-scious, thus indirectly offering a psychological basis for Marx's sociological analysis. Some Christian theologians of his day were irritated when told that the medieval Christian philosopher's *voluntas sequitur intellectum* would have to be revised in the light of Freud's clinical evidence. The will does not always follow but precedes the intellect and often even dictates terms to it. Freud demonstrated how one's options color one's thinking—how human reasoning slavishly serves our interests and legitimizes what we secretly or openly desire. What Freud examined at the level of individual consciousness, Marx had already discovered at the level of social consciousness—namely, that ideology is the implicit theory by which a dominant class justifies its privileged status. Both Freud and Marx seem to have gone further in pointing out that even religious theories often serve to legitimize vested interests.

The Buddha, who discovered the unconscious more than two millennia before Freud, also spoke of mental delusion (*moha*) and the veil of non-knowledge (*avijjā*) that keep truth from being apprehended by the human mind. In his vocabulary, the closest approximation to ideology in the pejora-tive sense was *diṭṭhi*, a partial and therefore deceptive formulation of the truth tenaciously clung to. Like Christian mystical tradition, as we shall see below, Buddhist spirituality too had foreseen the misuse of human reason. In the much misinterpreted *Kālāma Sutta*, the Buddha does not appear to be the nineteenth-century European rationalist that many contemporary writers try to make of him. There, he clearly rejected even logical reasoning as an adequate means of arriving at the truth. He saw too many persons being deceived by their own logic. Reason is that part of the human psyche that is prone to corruption by interest. The truth, in the ultimate sense for the Buddha, was beyond logical reasoning (*avitakkavacāra*). The only infallible way to reach the true knowledge of reality (*yathābhūtajñāna*) was to cut across human reason by penetrative insight (*vipassanā*), which itself could be ac-quired only after a long struggle against selfish interests that corrupt the human conscience and bind it with fetters. For the Buddha, even religion could be a psychic obsession enslaving the mind—he called it *silabbata-Parāmāsa*.

as Freud pointed,

Ideology and Sociology of Knowledge

This insight of the Buddha (and later of Freud) was also the central teaching in the mystical tradition of the Christian West. Every spirituality (and there were many) had developed a method of self-purification by which egocentric interests that cloud one's mind and consequently distort one's perception of reality were detected and eliminated. If we may use the term "ideology" anachronistically, we can say that every form of Christian spirituality con-tained an introspective analysis geared to the discovery of the truth free of all "ideological" projections. The mystic knew that the human psyche builds up various defense mechanisms to soften the harsh demands of the (Ultimate) Truth, for Truth always hurts before it liberates. From Evagrius Ponticus of the fourth century to Ignatius Loyola of the sixteenth, there was a continuous line of mystical tradition that provided serious seekers of the Ultimate Truth with various "tests" or "spiritual exercises" to forestall "vested interests" and remove "ideological blinkers." What Freud discovered on the couch, the mystics had also detected kneeling in their pews. It was the theologians sitting at their desks who did not see it immediately.

But all this was only at the psychological level of knowledge. What was not available to them, however, and is still unacceptable to otherwise holy men and women of our times, is the sociological perception of ideological biases, as Marx saw them. That social analysis must complement self-analysis in order to discern truth or reality in its totality is a fact still not palatable to religious persons. There is a naive theory among some religionists that if the individuals of a given society attain interior purity, the whole society would automatically become just. But this theory presupposes, falsely, that a society is simply the sum total of individuals. The truth is that if individual conversion is not accompanied by a corresponding structural change, the counterforces that operate in society overpower individuals in their efforts to attain the desired perfection.

By way of illustration, let me recount an interesting conversation that took place between two Buddhist monks at the multilateral dialogue organized by the World Council of Churches in 1974. The late Ven. Dr. Anada Thera put forward the traditional thesis by narrating the rather well-known story about the child who was asked to put together the torn pieces of a world map. The task was too difficult for her until she found a figure of a person sketched on the other side of the paper. She put the figure of the person aright and automatically the world map on the reverse side took its correct shape. "First put the person in order," concluded the learned Thera, "and the world too will come right." The applause hardly subsided when another monk, the Ven. Thic Nhat Hanh of Vietnam, who had seen the ravages of war and the power that unjust social structures wield over individual human beings, stood up and drew the attention of both the narrator and the audience to an unnoticed detail of the parable: not *any* picture of a person, when put right, automatically sets the world map right; but only the image of a person carrying the image of the world behind it! It is the person in dynamic relationship to society and not simply the person in isolation that needs to be put right, if we wish to put the world in order!

This means that a cultural revolution (which consists of attitudinal changes) must go hand in hand with a structural revolution. Even the Buddha, who laid a heavy accent on personal spirituality, also instituted a monastic structure as a framework conducive both for the individual and for the group to attain the ideal of *dhamma*, "doctrine," "truth." The great oversight of many Marxists is their underestimation of the need for personal spiritual growth in a world of collectivism. But this does not justify the other extreme to which some religionists are driven.

The psychology of knowledge that the religions have bequeathed to us, if complemented by a sociology of knowledge, can eliminate that species of ideological naivety characteristic of certain religious communities that live complacently in a socially unjust environment. It is heartening to note that the Asian (Catholic) monks who met in Kandy in 1980 for their third congress realized the need for a *sociological* perception of evil, which the monastic tradition regarded mainly as a *psychological* force. In doing so, they could not avoid a certain ideological frame of reference. It is worth quoting the following passage from their Final Statement, which was approved unanimously:

Our people's misery is not the result of an accident. It is man-made. It is the fruit of sinfulness, of oppressive social structures, of corruption in certain countries, and of an unjust international economic system. In large measure it is the consequence of the plundering of the world's natural resources by a minority which is getting richer, while the poor become poorer. In the same way as we ask our Asian communities to keep a critical eye on the established order, and when necessary to take up the defense of the poor against oppressors within their society, so we humbly wish to ask our brothers and sisters from rich countries to be more aware of the terrible responsibility borne by their countries for the poverty of our country and of their responsibility to awaken their fellow citizens' consciences. It is through contemplative prayer, first of all, that we recognize the cry of the poor. Yet we also need to undertake a serious, even scientific, analysis of the causes of poverty and of the various mechanisms that keep it in place.

CROSSING THE BOUNDARY

My final observation is that if ideology is a limitation, it certainly is a legitimate one. No idea however powerful, no vision however grand, no spirituality however liberating can effect any significant change in human history if it is not verbalized and systematized into an ideology or a religion. In fact, the Buddha's last "temptation" was precisely whether he should remain in his solitudinal bliss or go down to the people and communicate his message of deliverance. Had he chosen the first alternative, we would not be speaking of him here, and the history of Asia would have been very different. Once he decided to communicate his discovery, he had also to formulate it, thus giving rise to doctrinal discourse (*sutta*) and to a definite lifestyle (*vinaya*), neither of which supersedes the *dhamma* it is meant to express. Hence, the Buddha's own warning: the *dhamma* could be harmful just like a serpent, if it is "grasped" in the wrong way! Is this not tantamount to saying that *dhamma* should not be turned into a *diṭṭhi*—that is, an ideology in the wrong sense?

This is why the Buddha compares religious doctrine to a boat that, once the further shore is reached, ceases to be an asset and becomes a liability unless abandoned. All religions and ideologies need to be transcended by the truth they try to articulate. It is precisely on this point that both religionists and Marxists are divided within their own camps into traditionalists and revisionists.

Ideology is therefore ambivalent, just as is religion. It could run counter to the truth it wishes to incarnate. Or more concretely, we can speak of a liberating aspect of ideology (or religion) and an enslaving aspect. Though Marx was preoccupied with the enslaving dimension of ideology, it was soon recognized (particularly by Lenin) that ideology could also be a weapon of liberation in the hands of an enlightened proletariat. A parallel evolution is also noticed in Buddhist thought where *ditthi* had a pejorative connotation in the earliest strata of the canon but soon became a neutral concept that forked out into *sammā-ditthi* and *micchā-ditthi*, the one leading to interior freedom and the other to enslavement.

If there is right ideology and wrong ideology, then, "to be ideologically free" would mean opting for the right ideology rather than abandoning it altogether. It is a question of acquiring the right frame of mind, formulating the right questions, and so forth. This is so especially for those who do not postulate an absolute future or a further shore that by definition transcends and relativizes all ideologies, right or wrong. In this lies a basic difference between Marxism and religion.

Had Marx acknowledged an absolute future, or a further shore outside ideological categories, he would have crossed the boundary between religion and ideology. No transcendent, timeless, metacosmic future that escapes empirical verification appears even in the most speculative parts of his writings. But he did envisage what we might call a proximate and an ultimate future. His immediate interest was in the proximate future, which was to be born of the contradictions of a capitalist society and would, therefore, receive its birthmarks from that society. We presume that the socialist societies in Marxist regimes today correspond to the immediate future that Marx visualized; they certainly carry the stigmata of the bourgeois societies from which they issued.

Fully developed communism belonged, in Marx's thinking, to a further stage when all human alienations are expected to disappear. Such full emancipation of human society was the remote goal he strained his eyes to see. He glimpsed on the horizon a new humankind fully restored to itself, a fully developed social entity. Fear of falling prey to the visionary delusions of utopian socialists might have deterred him from making too many positive statements about it. Or was his silence due to the fact that it was an absolute future that seemed to lie beyond all empirical verifications? "Whereof one cannot speak, thereof one must be silent."

He also left unanswered the crucial question of whether the ultimate future would arise dialectically out of the contradictions of the proximate future— that is, from the postrevolutionary socialist societies (in which case, will the ultimate future show the birthmarks received from the contradictions of such societies?)—or whether this ultimate future was of such ultimacy as to imply a total rupture from the proximate future, with no sign of "birthmarks"?

This question is not purely speculative; rather, it is wholly political, as it practically amounts to asking whether this incomplete and defective stage of communism found in socialist countries today is going to remain unchanged! Does it have a built-in mechanism to bring about the next stage? Is another human revolution required to allow this ultimate future to dawn? Or is it a further shore that one must simply strive toward in faith and hope?

If these questions are not answered by Marx or his followers, they should at least be raised, because they spring from the ideological premises of Marxism itself. But, then, whoever frames these questions has already left the realm of ideology and entered that of faith! For Marxism is the kind of ideology that drives the inquisitive mind to the threshold of religion, for one's *faith* in the perfectibility of the present can be sustained only by a *hope* in a perfect future, and no future is perfect (or classless) if it is not one of unbounded *love*.

PART II

Religion and Liberation

4

Asia's Non-Semitic Religions and the Mission of Local Churches

PERSPECTIVES AND CLARIFICATIONS

Perspectives

Today's mission crisis is basically an authority crisis. It is well known that in the heart of the traditional churches that founded missions, the once all-pervasive authority of institutional leadership has been increasingly questioned or simply ignored. Those who wielded authority saw it as a crisis of obedience. To the rest it was a crisis of credibility. When this crisis matured in the colonial frontiers of the same churches—that is, in the so-called mission lands—it traveled back to the center in the guise of a mission crisis. As I see it, therefore, the mission crisis is no more and no less than an authority crisis.

In Asia, this crisis lay dormant for centuries until Vatican II fanned its embers into a conflagration of self-criticism leaving the Catholic Church's "missionary claims" in cinders. From these cremated remains we Asians are called upon to resurrect a new credible symbol of God's saving presence among our peoples, an authoritative word from a source of revelation universally recognized as such in Asia. In short, we are summoned to fashion the contours of a *new missionary community* truly qualified to announce God's kingdom and mediate the liberative revolution inaugurated by Jesus through his life and death—that is, a community that seeks no other sign of credibility or authority than that which such mediation would bestow upon it. What is asked of us, then, is nothing short of an *ecclesiological revolution*. The frontier situation in which we live has opened up a new horizon for us. Though our praxis is punctuated by debates and deliberations, we have no hesitation about the direction of our quest. The perspectives are clear and self-evident.

It is these perspectives that I wish to set forth here. They consist of assumptions that require no substantiation but need only to be explicated. I shall attempt to set up a framework of discussion by spelling out our missiological assumptions around the central concepts in the title of this chapter: "mission," "local church," and "religions."

Originally a lecture given at the SEDOS Seminar on "The Future of the Missions" in Rome, March 1981. First published in *The Month,* 15 (1982) 81-90.

1. The term "local church" is a tautology. For there is no church that is not local. And I hasten to add that there are Christian communities in Asia that are truly churches, and, therefore, authentically local.

2. This, however, does not imply that all local churches *in* Asia are necessarily local churches *of* Asia! Most of them, regrettably, are local churches of another continent struggling for centuries to get acclimatized to the Asian ethos. Obviously, I refer here to the so-called Western missions—Asian branches of local churches such as those of Rome, England, and so on. This applies in a limited way also to the Oriental Rite churches that can legitimately claim to be local churches of Asia—though, perhaps, not always of *today's* Asia! I confine my observations here to the former category—the Western missions.

3. My observations do not warrant the conclusion that the immediate task of local churches *in* Asia is to become local churches *of* Asia, and that this is an indispensable condition for the evangelization of Asian nations. That is a species of missiology lying beneath the theories of "inculturation." I do not uphold this view. I see the process of "becoming the local church *of* Asia" only as an accompaniment or a corollary to the process of "fulfilling the mission of evangelizing the (Asian) nations." Put conversely, it means that the local churches *in* Asia have not fulfilled their mission and therefore have failed to produce local churches *of* Asia.

4. Mission to the nations is primarily (Medellín, 1968), even if not exclusively (Puebla, 1980), mission to the *poor*. He who entrusted this mission to us has so defined it. Because good news to the poor is always bad news to the rich, the liberation of the rich is mediated by the liberation of the poor, not vice versa. Our mission, in other words, is prophetic and has been stamped from its inception with a class option. Hence the observation: a local church *in* Asia is usually a rich church working *for* the poor, whereas the local church *of* Asia could only be a poor church working *with* the poor, a church that has been evangelized, a church that has become good news to Asians.

5. This church, however, is a little flock, a tiny minority in Asia and has no monopoly of this mission. The *great* (monastic) *religions* that antedate Christianity also claim to possess a message of liberation for the poor of Asia. That is why local churches *in* Asia look upon these religions as rival claimants; but in a local church *of* Asia, they will have already become collaborators in a common mission.

6. The moment we associate the Asian poor and the Asian religions with our prophetic mission, we are right in the middle of *politics*. Moreover, poverty and religion are two areas where confrontation with two political ideologies—capitalism and Marxism—cannot be avoided. These two ideologies are directly involved with the "liberation" of the *Asian poor* and have definite theories about and attitudes toward *Asian religions*. The local church in Asia, whether prophetic or not, rich or poor, is a *political church*: a neutral church is a contradiction in terms, for it would not be local.

7. Inasmuch as all these religions and ideologies claim to be liberative

movements, saviors of the masses, *it is only the poor who decide who is competent to liberate them.* Neither textual proofs (our authority is mentioned in our holy books) nor the appeal to tradition (we always claimed this authority and people used to accept it) are adequate today. *Authority is the spontaneous manifestation of a church's competence to mediate total liberation for the peoples of Asia.* The ultimate source of this authority is he who entrusted the mission to us. But he has identified himself with the poor as the "victim-judge" (Matt. 25) and it is in and through the poor that the church or any other religion or ideology will receive this authority here in Asia. The *authority crisis* therefore remains a *permanent possibility* in the mission of a local church in Asia.

Clarifications

The political implications of this prophetic mission constitute only one source of conflicts that local churches experience today. Another major divisive factor that can be eliminated more easily is found purely in the area of semantics. The key words "religion" and "poverty," which together describe the Asian ethos, are themselves polysemous words, signifying contradictory realities. Those engaged in missiological debates—especially the "liberationists" and "inculturationists"—are both guilty of oversimplifying this complex question.

It is curious that even the Medellín documents, when speaking of the phenomenon of "poverty," take a zigzag path, now deploring it, now counting its blessings. The ambiguity can be traced back to the Gospels. When Jesus invited the rich young man to sell all things and give (not, of course, to the temple, but) to the poor, he required the rich man not to be rich and the poor not to be poor! The Marian manifesto in Luke announces the messianic intervention whereby the positions of the rich and the poor would be reversed, implying that both riches and poverty be eliminated.

The attempt to distinguish "economic" from "evangelical" poverty does not help clear this ambiguity. The only way out would be to admit a distinction between "forced poverty," inflicted on some by the hedonism or the indifference of others (Dives and Lazarus), and "voluntary poverty" embraced as a protest and a precaution against "forced poverty." The one is enslaving; the other is liberating. In Eastern religions, voluntary poverty is a spiritual antidote against the mammon working in humanity psychologically. In liberation theology, it is also a sociological weapon—that is, a political strategy— necessary in the battle against the organized selfishness of the principalities and powers of mammon. Mahatma Gandhi is the most outstanding Asian example of voluntary poverty with both its psychological and sociological implications.

A similar clarification is desirable in the understanding of "religion." Under the influence of a Marxist critique of religion, and the biblical hermeneutics of Latin American theologians, some of our Asian liberationists define religion and poverty as negative forces forming an unholy alliance from which the

Asian masses have to be liberated. Poverty for them is an evil in itself. Religion is said to perpetuate it, first by restricting the area of spiritual liberation to the nonsocial, nonpolitical, noneconomic plane (where would such a plane be?), and secondly by legitimizing—as well as allowing itself to be legitimized by— oppressive systems that create and maintain the evils of poverty.

Inculturationists, on the other hand, ignore or gloss over this negative aspect of religion and sometimes of poverty, except perhaps when they acknowledge the failure of *other* religions to inspire a Mother Teresa who would alleviate the sufferings of the poor! The demand for radical transformation of society as an indispensable condition for the elimination of suffering is neutralized by "apostolic works," which turn victims of poverty into perpetual objects of compassion. They also appreciate the monastic thrust of major Asian religions in that these religions value poverty as something to be voluntarily embraced in order to combat selfishness and acquisitiveness. They would want the church to absorb these traits of various religions in becoming more "at home" in Asia. But this approach of the inculturationists sounds too accommodative to liberationists.

The reality is more complex. Religion, too, has an enslaving and a liberating dimension as much as does poverty. After all, has not the same Christian religion produced a theology of domination and a theology of liberation?

I draw out, in Table 1, the contradictory realities that the words "religion" and "poverty'" designate. They show that these words are bipolar, each containing a negative and a positive role. And each pole has two complementary dimensions: sociological and psychological—or more precisely, sociopolitical and individual. I hope the ensuing discussion of concrete issues will become clearer in the light of this fourfold distinction.

CONCRETE ISSUES

Inculturation, Indigenous Theology, and Oriental Spirituality

Inculturation is something that happens naturally. It can never be induced artificially. A Christian community tends to appropriate the symbols and mores of the human groupings around it only to the degree that it immerses itself in their lives and struggles. That is to say, inculturation is the by-product of an *involvement* with a people rather than the conscious target of a program of action. For it is a people that creates a culture. It is, therefore, from the people with whom one becomes involved that one understands and acquires a culture.

The questions that are foremost in the minds of inculturationists are, therefore, totally irrelevant—namely, whether a particular church is inculturated or not, or why it is not inculturated, and how it could be inculturated. Yet it is relevant to know why such irrelevant questions are asked so frequently in our local churches today. My diagnosis is that the inculturationists are starting off from the observation, valid in itself, that the ecclesiastical culture of the

Table 1

The Bipolarity of Religion and Poverty

Poles	Dimensions	
	Psychological (individual)	Sociological (socio-political)
The enslaving face of religion	Superstition, ritualism, dogmatism, etc.; transcendentalism (= Manichaeism, Docetism, etc.)	Tendency of religion to legitimize an oppressive status quo = tendency of religion to serve mammon, anti-God; commercialism
The liberating face of religion	Interior liberation from sin (= mammon, anti-God,*tanhā* ["greed"], exploitive instincts)	Organizational and motivational potential of religion for radical social change (e.g., independence movements in Asia)
The enslaving face of poverty	Imposed poverty violating the dignity of the human person (alienation)	Poverty as the subjugation of peoples by the slaves of mammon (= disinheritance, dispossession, etc., through colonization, multinational corporations, etc.)
The liberating face of poverty	Voluntary poverty as one's interior liberation from mammon— i.e., a *spiritual antidote* (emphasized by Eastern religions)	Voluntary poverty as a *political strategy* in the liberation of human society from mammon, organized sin (stance of liberation theologians)

ministerial church in Asia is elitist and stands aloof from the culture of the impoverished masses. This cultural gap is even more pronounced in former European colonies—India, Malaysia, or Indo-China—where seminary training and all clerical communication is done in the language of former colonial masters. But what the inculturationists fail to perceive is that the *cultural gap* has an *economic base*; that the church's twofold culture indicates a sociological process in which the *class division* of the wider society has been ecclesiologically registered in the life of the believing community—a sin against the body of the Lord, as St. Paul would have it; that clerical culture represents the *dominant sector* of the believing community.

Moreover, the irrelevance of the above-mentioned questions, which is at the center of the inculturation debate, is rooted in the erroneous presupposition that churches in Asia are not inculturated. But every local church, being itself a people, is essentially an inculturated church. The relevant question to ask, therefore, is: *Whose culture* does the official church reflect? Which is the same as asking, *What social class* is the church predominantly associated with? Do the poor—the principal addressees of the good news and the special invitees to Christian discipleship—constitute a culturally decisive factor in the local church? Thus the whole inculturation issue derives its significance from the local church's basic mission to bring—and *become*—the good news to the poor in Asia.

Incidentally, the current discussion on indigenization, if situated in the context of this basic mission, would require that we review critically the instruments of apostolate most local churches are using for the training of ministers (that is, the seminaries) and for the education of the laity (schools, colleges, technological institutes). Are these not the institutions that perpetuate the aforesaid cultural gap by maintaining the class division lying beneath it? Did they not originate in an era when evangelization was restricted to mean a quantitative extension of an already stratified ecclesiastical complex with no idea of the *ecclesiological revolution* that "evangelization" always evokes?

In the contemporary church, this ecclesiological revolution seems to have begun with the mushrooming of "basic communities" or grassroot communities or *ecclesiolae*. In the next section of this chapter I shall indicate the specific contribution that Asia offers to this revolution. Suffice it here merely to record that the growth of such apostolic communes coincides with a reevangelization of the church as a whole, the evolution of new ministries, and the formation of new ministers within the cultural ethos of the poor, and the reawakening of the poor themselves to their irreplaceable role in the liberative revolution that Jesus referred to as the kingdom. One bishop in Sri Lanka has to his credit at least four ministers formed outside the traditional seminary. A second group has begun training. I, too, am engaged in a similar project. Indeed, there are a few laboratories of hope where the Christ-experience of the less privileged comes to be spontaneously formulated into an indigenous theology.

If, however, this last observation is valid—namely, that an indigenous theology in our context is an articulation of the Christ-experience of Asia's poor—then neither the clerical leadership of the church nor even the Asian (liberation) theologians who have been educated in an elitist culture can claim to be the engineers of an indigenous theology. In fact, like the hierarchical church, these theologians, too, speak of the poor in the third person! This is an implicit acknowledgment that they are not really poor. On the other hand, the poor have not yet been truly evangelized and they, too, are not, therefore, qualified as yet to spell out an indigenous theology for Asia. They have only received the *seed* of liberation from the gospel and from other religions—the "positive pole" of religion, as I called it earlier. *To evangelize Asia, in other words, is to evoke in the poor this liberative dimension of Asian religiousness, Christian and non-Christian.* For the unevangelized poor tend to reduce religion to an opiate, to struggle without hope, and to submit too easily to the religious domination of the elite class.

The Asian dilemma, then, can be summed up as follows: the theologians are not (yet) poor; and the poor are not (yet) theologians! This dilemma can be resolved only in the local churches *of Asia*—that is, in the grassroot communities where the theologians and the poor become culturally reconciled through a process of mutual evangelization. This reciprocal exposure to the gospel consists in this, that the *theologians are awakened into the liberative dimension of poverty and the poor are conscientized into the liberative potentialities of their religiousness.* Thus, if there is any model of a local church for Asians, it should be in those Asian communities where the positive poles of religion and poverty merge; and such communities do exist in Asia outside the Christian churches, and to these I shall turn my attention in the next section of this chapter.

This said, I consider it a waste of time even to comment on the efforts of those scholars who employ their knowledge of ancient religious texts to build up conceptual frameworks for an "indigenous theology" that the poor have no need of. I, myself a classical Indologist, do not deny that the sacred texts contain the nucleus around which contemporary Asian religion has evolved. But to draw an indigenous theology from ancient texts without allowing the practice of religion to play its hermeneutical role in the interpretation of those very texts is to make the cart pull the horse.

It is more profitable to discuss the efforts of those who concentrate on *Oriental spirituality* as the locus of an indigenous theology. This term seems to stand for what I have described here as the positive (that is, liberative) pole of Asian religion. It is a whole way of being and seeing that one acquires when the inner core of one's personality (variously called "mind," "heart," "soul," "consciousness," etc.) is radically transformed by means of an asceticism of renunciation. Its aim is to free the human person of the ego, cleanse it of its innate thirst for power over others, and purify it of its propensity for acquisitiveness. It is a psychological process by which one experiences an interior liberation from mammon, to use a biblical idiom.

In this matter there are, I suggest, four pitfalls to avoid. The first is that indigenization should not amount in practice to that species of "theological vandalism" by which, all too often, Oriental techniques of introspection are pulled out of the soteriological ethos of Eastern religions and made to "serve"

Christian prayer with no reverence for the wholeness of non-Christians' religious experience. I protested against this insensitiveness at the Asian Theological Conference in 1979 and I reiterate it here, offering at the same time an alternative approach that respects the self-understanding of other religions (see the next section).

The second warning is that any tendency to create or perpetuate a "leisure class" through "prayer centers" and "ashrams" that attract the more affluent to short spells of mental tranquility rather than to a life of renunciation, is an abuse of Oriental spirituality. To turn Asian religious experience into an opiate that deadens the conscience of both the rich and the poor vis-à-vis their respective stations in life is unevangelical. The positive pole of Asian religiousness has to synchronize with the positive role of poverty. It is the hallmark of an Asian religion to evoke in its adherents a desire to renounce the ego and abandon the worship of mammon—indeed a fine complement to Jesus' messianic mission to the poor, which the church claims to continue in Asia.

Commercialism is the third danger on the list. What used to happen to our material resources like tea, copper, wood, or oil, is now happening to our spiritual treasures. They go West, thanks to the conspiracy of merchants and missioners, and return attractively processed . . . to be sold back to us for our own consumption. Local agents of exploitation are most to be blamed. Some of our maharishis and roshis from Asia have turned meditation into a veritable dollar-spinner! Transcendental Meditation or T.M. is an example of how an Oriental product has returned to Asia after being processed into a sophisticated product of the West. Such imported goods seem more respectable in the eyes of most clerics and religious of Asian origin.

Being of an elitist stock by training, they recoil from consulting the authentic sources of Oriental spirituality to be found at their very door step. After all, they belong to the local church of another continent, as explained earlier. Many ecclesiastical superiors, quite understandably, find these processed goods "safer" for their subjects. The challenge that the original religiousness of Asia presents to the church is thus neutralized. Even renewal programs sometimes are so developed as to keep participants from being drawn into the spiritual mines of Asia.

My fourth and final remark is about the conscious or unconscious motives that inspire spiritual dialogues with other religions. I suspect that the spiritual sharing of religious insights is often advocated as a strategy against a common enemy, be it secularism or consumerism, atheism or communism. The Christian obligation to make an open attack on the principalities and powers that build altars to mammon—for what else is atheism and consumerism?—is carefully replaced by an excessive zeal for intramural sharing of spiritual patrimonies among selected groups of religionists. The emphasis seems to be put on the "negative pole" of Asian religion. Regrettably, therefore, so-called Oriental spirituality is endorsed in Christian circles as an *apolitical escape* from complex human situations, rather than allowed to burst forth as a *prophetic movement* against the organized sin that keeps Asia poor.

Asian Religions and the Politics of Poverty in the Context of the Local Church's Mission to the Poor

Poverty is not just a socio-economic condition of the Asian masses; it is also a political reality. Marxists claim that religion thrives on it. Capitalists claim that Marxism capitalizes on it. *Both* Marxists *and* capitalists are busy with the politics of poverty. Religion, which has its own theory of poverty, is caught in between. It is in the midst of these politico-religious ambiguities that the local churches *in* Asia are called to exercise their prophetic mission to the poor. Evangelization takes place always within or against but never outside a given political system.

I might suggest that in this forest of conflicts we can see a clear path opened before us here in Asia, thanks to its ancient tradition of *religious socialism*. Before I describe this phenomenon, let me define the term "socialism." Because it is a loaded word, I wish to restrict its meaning to the theory and praxis of social organization in which the means of production are owned by a whole community and the fruits of labor are distributed among its members equitably. The principle of justice involved here is expressed best in the famous Marxian adage: "To each according to need; from each according to ability." In a way, this seems to be the norm that an average human family of any culture adheres to. Why I call this phenomenon "religious" will become evident as I try to describe it.

There are actually two clear versions of religious socialism in Asia: (1) the more primitive form practiced by the *clannic* and quasiclannic societies spread throughout the vast stretches of nonurbanized Asia, and (2) the more sophisticated form represented by the *monastic* communities of Buddhist (Hindu, Taoist) origin. The clannic society is known to anthropologists as pretechnological (I prefer to say pretechnocratic), and its belief system is described as "animism"—a word I prefer to replace with the more appropriate phrase, *cosmic religiousness*, in order to include also refined religious expressions such as Shintoism and Confucianism. In this system the order of nature and the order of society overlap; social harmony is insured by cosmic communion with the elements of nature. The communism of Asian monks, on the other hand, is founded on a *metacosmic religiousness* that points to a salvific beyond attainable within the person through gnosis; it inculcates, not a negation of cosmic reality as is often erroneously thought, but a "nonaddiction to cosmic needs." However, the origin and early development of this system has been historically associated with feudalism that came to be superimposed on clannic societies.

Note, therefore, that the two species of socialism belong to different social systems (clannic and feudal) and to different religious systems (cosmic and metacosmic). The relationship between the two varies according to regions. There could be—and not seldom there are—contradictions between the two. The monastic community may practice perfect communism within its own membership but could act as a feudal lord toward clannic societies. After all, has not history proved that a socialist nation can be exploitive with regard to other countries? The monastic life has often succumbed to this weakness wherever it is maintained by, and therefore made to legitimize, feudal (and now, capitalist) regimes. What the monks own in common and share equitably could very well be the property of clannic societies, expropriated by political regimes that seek religious sanction from the monks. Thus, contemplative life supposedly based on "voluntary poverty" could be the luxury of a leisure class maintained by the "really poor."

This, incidentally, is why I warned "Oriental spirituality enthusiasts" not to foster a feudal or leisure-class mentality, and why I have urged the indigenizers of theology to become poor, and the inculturationists to get involved with the masses.

This contradiction between the way monks share land and its fruits, and the way rural societies share land and labor, seems to fade into a happy symbiosis in some of the least urbanized, least technocratized areas of Asia. Monks supported by alms live in remote villages in the framework of a religious socialism that knows no cultural or economic gap between the monastic community and the village community. Religion is not made to justify a class division, even if the monk remains a soteriological symbol and a spiritual guide set apart and above the common folk.

This phenomenon may not be as widespread or as permanent as we should like it to be, for there are hostile influences eroding it both from within Asian cultures (e.g., feudalism) and from without (e.g., capitalist technocracy). Nevertheless, in this we have an Asian model of a basic community. Here poverty—even economic poverty—seems to acquire an evangelical flavor because it is practiced "voluntarily" for the good of the community. I seek to be satisfied with what I really *need* but give all I *can* to the community. In *rural socialism*, the earth is everybody's property and nobody's monopoly. In *monastic socialism*, cosmic needs are made to serve rather than obsess the person. This is a religious conviction, a salvific path. It is a system in which poverty and religion conspire to liberate humanity from "cosmic obsessions"—for which urbanized Asians have learned another name: "consumerism."

Reinforcing the conclusions of my previous arguments, I suggest that, if the local church's point of insertion in the Asian ethos is the multiplication of grassroot apostolic communities, then Asia offers fresh motives for creating them and holds up its own indigenous mold to cast them in. Inculturation? This is where it happens. Indigenization? This is its only source. Oriental spirituality? This is its finest societal expression. The ecclesiological revolution we so eagerly await as a prelude to inculturation and indigenization is none other than an evangelical response to the promises that religious socialism of Asia offers our local churches today.

In fact, great political leaders of Asia saw in it a great political and social antidote against capitalism, consumerism and, of course, feudalism, which has not yet vanished from Asia. The Sarvodaya Movement, as originally envisaged by Mahatma Gandhi and organized by Vinobha Bhave, was founded on this conviction. Mao Tse Tung and, more particularly, Ho Chi Minh recognized in the peasant mentality both an ingrained capacity for a socialist reconstruction of society and a natural inclination for acquisitiveness. The struggle between grace and sin, God and mammon, is never absent in Asia. This is what makes our adoption of rural socialism both a religious imperative and a political option.

If the local church *in* Asia dismisses this idea as utopian, it is precisely because that church is not *of* Asia but is a monarchical or feudal establishment of another continent, now seeking desperately to be "inculturated"—after having failed for centuries to strike roots in Asia. It once linked evangelization with colonization, and it now offers us a capitalist, technocratic model of "human" development as "preevangelization"! Even this criticism is severely censured by it. Recently, the European central authority of a local church planted here four hundred years ago reprimanded Asian theologians for criticizing capitalism! Even in the official documents in which this church questions the values of this atheistic system, one does not often hear it "calling the devil by his name"—to use an Asian idiom for exorcism, for it sees a greater threat in Marxism, which is becoming a rival religion in the Third World.

Marxist states, to be sure, are confessionalist and give no official recognition to any view of life or code of behavior other than their own. Thus when the church faces established Marxism, it sees, as in a mirror, its own authoritarianism and dogmatism, its own reluctance to give autonomy to local communities on the periphery, and its own maneuvers to centralize power. What is more, if the church hesitates to challenge capitalism openly, because it is indirectly associated with its institutions, it cannot also condemn Marxist atrocities in Asia without recalling its own colonial centuries, which have left indelible scars on entire nations.

This dilemma of the church in Asia is further accentuated by the fact that the time and energy wasted on theoretical battles against Marxism is not more fruitfully devoted to the practical task of joining Asia's own war against injustice and exploitation. Such a church is not prepared to appreciate or foster Asian socialism, because of political implications. To sum up then: the first and the last word about the local church's mission to the poor of Asia is total identification (or "baptismal immersion," as I am about to call it in the next part of this chapter) with monks and peasants who have conserved for us, in their *religious socialism*, the seeds of liberation that *religion* and *poverty* have combined to produce. It is the one sure path opened for the local church to remove the cross from the steeples where it has stood for four centuries and plant it once more on Calvary where the prophetic communities die victims of politics and religion in order to rise again as local churches *of* Asia. It is this death and resurrection that I wish to discuss in the third and final part of this chapter.

THE WAY TOWARD ECCLESIOLOGICAL REVOLUTION: THE DOUBLE BAPTISM IN ASIAN RELIGION AND POVERTY

The Jordan of Asian Religion

Schillebeeckx has drawn our attention to the fact that the baptism under John was Jesus' first prophetic gesture, the memory of which became a source of lasting embarrassment to the first generation of Christians. The embarrassment lay in the fact that Jesus, whom his followers had come to worship as the Lord and the Christ, had thought it fit to begin his messianic mission by becoming himself a follower of John the Baptizer. The ecclesiological implications of this christological event have not been sufficiently appreciated in the contemporary church. I wish, therefore, to draw from it at least four missiological principles for the local church *in* Asia.

In the first place, I observe that Jesus was faced with several streams of traditional religiousness when he answered his prophetic call. Not every kind of religion appealed to him. From his later reactions we gather that the narrow ideology of the Zealot movement did not attract him. Nor did the sectarian puritanism of the Essenes have any impact on him. As for the Pharisaic spirituality of self-righteousness, Jesus openly ridiculed it. His confrontations with the Sadducees—the chief priests and elders—indicate that he hardly approved their aristocratic "leisure-class" spirituality. Rather, it was in the ancient (Deuteronomic) tradition of prophetic asceticism represented by the Baptizer that Jesus discovered an authentic spirituality and an appropriate point of departure for his own prophetic mission. In opting for this form of *liberative* religiousness to the exclusion of others, which appeared enslaving, he indulged in a species of "discernment," which we Christians in Asia, confronted with a variety of ideological and religious trends, are continually invited to make.

Secondly, we can immediately sense in this event a peculiar reciprocity between John's own personal spirituality and that of his followers. The Baptizer represented a "world-renouncing" spirituality of an extreme sort. We are told that he lived "with nature" rather than "in society"; his diet and his dress—things picked up from the desert—were symbolic of this brand of hermetical asceticism. But the Baptizer did not impose it on the baptized. The latter were the simple and the humble, the "religious poor" of the countryside, the ostracized but repentant sinners, the *anawim* who were drawn by his preaching and his lifestyle to be ever more receptive to the good news of imminent liberation. Thus, the poor, too, had a "spirituality" of their own.

It was, therefore, at the Jordan when Jesus stood before the Baptizer and among the baptized, that the two streams of spirituality found a point of confluence. Jesus, himself about to pass through a wilderness-experience of hermetical asceticism, comes to John—not to baptize others, but to be baptized, thus identifying himself with the "religious poor" of the countryside.

The ecclesiological implication of this christological event is very obvious. Asian local churches have a mission to be at the point of intersection between the metacosmic spirituality of the monastic religions and the cosmic religion of the simple peasants, to be the locus where the liberative forces of both traditions combine in such a way as to exclude the aristocratic leisure-class mentality of the former and superstitions of the latter. This is a missionary method we learn from Jesus.

The third principle I wish to enunciate here has to do with the "loss of authority" to which I reduced the current crisis of mission. Jesus' first prophetic gesture—like every other prophetic word and deed—is "self-authenticating." The prophet speaks and acts in God's name and with God's authority. If an event does not reveal this authority, then it is not prophetic. Jesus' humble submission to John's baptism, embarrassing as it was to early Christians, appeared to them, all the same, as a public manifestation of his *authority* to preach God's liberating reign about to dawn on the *anawim*. It was with this act of humility that his credibility was certified by God in the presence of the poor: *"Hear ye him."* It was a prophetic moment precisely because it was then that both his messianic self-understanding and his missionary credentials before the people were bestowed on him. Would that the local church in Asia were as humble as its spouse and Lord! Would that we Christians seek to be baptized rather than baptize!

The "fulfillment theory" of the church fathers now revived by Vatican II—which I have repeatedly criticized in the past—relegates other religions to a "pre-Christian" category of spirituality to be "fulfilled" through the church's missionary endeavor. It is on the basis of this theory that some (Western) missiologists speak of the need to "baptize" pre-Christian religions and cultures rather than of the prophetic imperative to immerse oneself in the baptismal waters of Asian religions that predate Christianity. The local church *in* Asia needs yet to be "initiated" into the pre-Christian traditions under the tutelage of our ancient gurus, or it will continue to be an ecclesiastical complex full of "power" but lacking in "authority." It is only in the Jordan of Asian religiousness that it will be acknowledged as a voice worthy of being heard by all: *"Hear ye him."*

The mission crisis is solved only when the church is baptized in the twofold liberative tradition of monks and peasants of Asia. Like its own Master, let it sit at the feet of Asian gurus not as an *ecclesia docens* (a teaching church) but as an *ecclesia discens* (a learning church), lost among the "religious poor" of Asia, among the *anawim* who go to their gurus in search of the kingdom of holiness, justice, and peace. The many individual attempts made in this direction are but symbolic beginnings. Unless the institutional church takes the plunge itself, it can hardly hope to be for Asians a readable word of revelation or a credible sign of salvation.

The fourth missiological principle comes as a response to the "problem of identity" that the third principle evokes. There is a phobia both in the West and in the (Western) local churches *in* Asia that all this represents a serious threat to the Christian identity of a believing community. A closer look shows that the roots of this phobia lie in the difficult option we have to make between a clear past and an unclear future—between the local churches *in* Asia with a clearly Western identity and the local churches *of* Asia with a yet unarticulated Asian identity. Further, in the model of the past, Western identity overlaps with Christian identity, and so in the church of the future one desires quite rightly that "Asianness" coincide with "Christianness." Christian identity never exists per se as a kind of neutral quantity from which Western elements could be drained and Asian features added! This comes from the very nature of a local church—which is at once church and local.

In this, as in everything else, the church must return to its source: Jesus Christ, who has enunciated for us the principle of losing oneself in order to find oneself. The clearest example is his baptism in the Jordan. This is precisely the fourth missiology principle. Was it not by losing his identity among the humble but repentant sinners and the "religious poor" of his country that he discovered—for himself and for others around him—his authentic selfhood: the lamb of God who liberates us from sin, the beloved Son to be listened to, the Messiah who had a new message and a new baptism to offer?

John's spirituality was traditional but negative; Jesus' was positive and entirely new. To John's curses on self-righteous religious bigots and political leaders, Jesus would add the blessings and promises offered to the marginalized poor and the ostracized sinner. The Baptizer preached bad news about the coming judgment, but Jesus, whom he baptized, had good news to give about imminent liberation. The precursor was conferring baptism of water on converts. The beloved Son would rather have the baptism of the cross conferred on himself for the conversion of the world. The one would question the belief that salvation came simply by membership in the chosen community and ask for individual conversion, but the other would change the people so converted into a community of love.

Yes, there would be a radical change also in the lifestyle that Jesus chose in contrast with John's. The Baptizer came without eating and drinking; the Son of Man would go to parties in the company of sinners. Thus plunging himself into the stream of an ancient spirituality, he came out with his own new mission. It is baptism alone that confers on us our Christian identity and the Christian newness we look for in Asia. Does not the fear of losing its identity keep the local church from discovering it? Does not the fear of dying keep it from living? The newness of Asian Christianity will appear only as a result of our total participation in the life and aspirations of the religious poor of Asia, the *anawim* of Asia.

The Calvary of Asian Poverty

The trajectory of poverty that links Jordan with Calvary is the other missiological paradigm that I wish our local churches *in* Asia would reflect upon. I have already noted that, of all the religious currents of Israel, only the Johannine stream of spirituality appeared truly liberative in Jesus' judgment. John had renounced wealth and power so radically that he had immense *authority* before the religious poor of Israel to speak in God's name. Authority is always associated with poverty, not with power. In fact, at his preaching those who wielded power lost their authority. They killed him in rage (Matt. 14:1–12). The lesson was clear: only those who are radically poor are qualified to preach the kingdom, and only those who are poor are disposed to receive it. God and mammon are enemies.

After being initiated into Johannine asceticism, Jesus is said to have had a decisive confrontation with wealth, power, and prestige: three temptations that he conquered by means of three renunciations (Matt. 4:1–11). Jesus, the laborer's son (Matt. 13:55) who had no place of his own to be born (Luke. 2:7), would from then onward have no place of his own to lay his head (Matt. 8:20), or even to be buried (Matt. 27:60). Jesus would go much further than John. His poverty was not merely a negative protest, not just a passive solidarity with the religious poor of Israel. It was a calculated strategy against mammon whom he declared to be God's rival (Matt. 6:24). The kingdom he announced was certainly not for the rich (Luke 6:20–26). It takes a miracle for a rich person to give up wealth and enter the kingdom (Mark 10:26–27). His curses on the "haves" (Luke 6:24–25) and his blessings on the "have-nots" (Luke 6:20–23) are sharpened by his dictum that it is in and through the poor (the hungry, the naked, etc.) that he would pass his messianic judgment on entire nations (Matt. 25:31–46).

No wonder that the very sight of money polluting religion made him resort to physical violence (John 2:13–17), for his mission was a prophetic mission—that is, a mission of the poor and a mission to the poor, a mission *by* the poor and a mission *for* the poor. This is the truth about evangelization that the local churches *in* Asia find hardest to accept. To awaken the consciousness of the poor to their unique liberative role in the totally new order God is about to usher in—this is how I have already defined evangelization—is the inalienable task of the poor already awakened. Jesus was the first evangelizer—poor but fully conscious of his part in the war against mammon with all its principalities and powers.

And it was this mission that was consummated on the cross—a cross that the money-polluted religiosity of his day planted on Calvary with the aid of a colonial power (Luke 23:1–23). This is where the journey, begun at Jordan, ended. When true religion and politics join hands to awaken the poor, then mammon, too, makes allies with religion and politics to conspire against the evangelizer. Religion and politics must go together—whether *for* God or *against* God.

It is, then, not without reason that the evangelists related Jesus' first prophetic gesture at the Jordan to his last prophetic gesture on Calvary by using the same word to describe both: baptism (Matt. 3:13–15; Mark 10:35–40; Luke 12:50). Each was a self-effacing act that revealed his prophetic *authority*. At the first baptism he was acknowledged as the beloved Son. At the second baptism the evangelist heard even the colonial power that killed him proclaim that he was truly a son of God (Mark 15:39)—indeed a prophetic moment, when humiliation gave birth to an exaltation capable of gathering a prophetic community, as the fourth Gospel teaches (John 12:32–33).

The baptism of the cross, therefore, is not only the price he paid for preaching the good news, but the basis of *all Christian discipleship* (Mark 8:34). Thus the threefold missionary mandate to *preach, baptize*, and *make disciples*—understood in the past as the juridical extension of one local church's power over other localities through a rite of initiation—must be redeemed of its narrow ecclesiocentric interpretation by tracing it back to the cross, the final proof of authentic *preaching*, the only true *baptism* that gives meaning to the sacrament that goes by that name, and the criterion of true Christian *discipleship*.

This cross we have now had for centuries in Asia. It was Fulton J. Sheen—a missiologist of quite another era—who said that the West seeks a Christ without the cross whereas the East has a cross without Christ! This judgment on the East is not quite exact. If there is no Christ without a cross, as Sheen supposes, could there be a cross without Christ? Can humanity ever put asunder what God has put together: Christ and the cross?

The cross that I speak of—a symbol of shame—is the one that a mercantile Christianity planted here with the aid of foreign powers. It is on this cross that the Asian poor are being baptized today! The unholy alliance of the missionary, the military, and the merchant of a previous era now continues with greater subtlety, for the local churches so planted *in* Asia, being still local churches *of* former colonizing countries, now continue their alliance with neocolonialism in order to survive; thus they cause the class division in the church mentioned earlier in the second section of this chapter. The colonial school system of the great missionary era has now given way to "development projects"—which of course advocate a theory of development that "developed countries" evolved in the very process of causing underdevelopment! It is the new form of "preevangelization."

Now development is giving way to "liberation"—in the same climate of Christian megalomania. A small minority church claims to offer "liberation" to Asia without first entering into liberative streams of Asian religion, which has its own antidotes against mammon. A sixteenth-century brand of Latin Christianity, which was "inculturated"—that is, given a light dusting of Asianness—after being in the Orient for four centuries as the one redemptive agent of God, now wants to "liberate" Asia without allowing Asia to liberate it of its Latinity! Hence, my final appeal to the local churches *in* Asia: Harden not your heart; enter into the stream at the point where the *religiousness of the Asian poor* (represented by the masses) and the *poverty of religious Asians* (reflected in our monks) meet to form the ideal community of total sharing, the "religious socialism" that, like the early Christian communism, can be swallowed up in the jungle of Asian feudalism as well as Western ideologies and theologies.

The prophetic communities that have arisen as a result of being baptized consciously or unconsciously into Asian socialism are now on the trajectory of poverty linking Jordan to Calvary. It is they who speak with *authority* in Asia; it is they who are the credible words of revelation, the readable signs of salvation, effective instruments of liberation. They are the true local churches *of* Asia, for they have been baptized in the Jordan of Asian religion and on the Calvary of Asian poverty. Until they are officially recognized as local churches *of* Asia, the authority crisis will continue in the local churches *in* Asia.

5

Western Models of Inculturation: Applicable in Asia?

Had St. Paul founded a church in Benares, Bangkok, or Beijing, and had he written an epistle to the Christians there, we would have had some scriptural norm or some kind of apostolic tradition to follow in forging our ecclesial identity in the non-Semitic cultures of Asia. Granted that the early church might have had some such experience in the case of the "St. Thomas Christians" in Kerala or the Nestorians in Central Asia, the fact remains that the doctrines and opinions articulated as the authoritative tradition of the early church were almost exclusively born of its encounter with the Semitic and the Greco-Roman worlds, and not with Sino-Indian religiousness. Most Asian churches have no precedent to follow. They are called upon to create something new, the orthodoxy of which cannot be gauged from the available models.

THE GRECO-ROMAN MODELS OF INCULTURATION: NOT APPLICABLE IN ASIA

The europeanization of Christianity, which accompanied the christianization of Europe is, *in itself*, an excellent paradigm of indigenization. It reveals at least four strands of tradition:

1. the Latin model: incarnation in a non-Christian *culture*
2. the Greek model: assimilation of a non-Christian *philosophy*
3. the North European model: accommodation to a non-Christian *religiousness*
4. the monastic model: participation in a non-Christian *spirituality*

These models are listed in the ascending order of their relevance in Asia. Strangely enough, the two standard examples cited in support of inculturation since De Nobili and Ricci are the first two, the Latin and the Greek, which, in my opinion, are the least applicable in contemporary Asia. I have at least four reasons for saying this.

First published in *Lumière et Vie,* 168 [1984] 50-62 whose editor had requested a summary of the author's views on the question of inculturation. First English publication appeared in *East Asian Pastoral Review,* 22 (1985) 116-24.

First, the "theology of religions" that permeates the Latino-Hellenistic tradition is unhelpful in Asia, besides being incompatible with the perspectives of Vatican II. The patristic tradition was consistently negative in its assessment of other religions, perhaps for valid reasons.[1] In the judgment of the church fathers, only the *culture* of Rome and the *philosophy* of Greece were worth being assumed by the church—that is, capable of being redeemed by Christ from the diabolical grip of pagan religion. Thus they seem to have initiated a "Christ-against-religion theology," which dominated Christian thought for centuries (not excluding that of De Nobili and Ricci), until some Indians (both Christian and Hindu) of the last century sowed the first seeds of a "Christ-of-religions theology."[2] This theology has appeared in a mitigated form in the documents of Vatican II and is being developed further in the writings of recent popes.[3]

Secondly, the separation of religion from culture (as in Latin Christianity) and religion from philosophy (as in Hellenic Christianity) makes little sense in an Asian society. In the South Asian context, for instance, culture and religion are overlapping facets of one indivisible soteriology, which is at once a view of life and a path of deliverance; it is both a philosophy that is basically a religious vision, and a religion that is a philosophy of life.[4]

The very word "inculturation," which is of Catholic origin and inspiration,[5] is based on this culture-religion dichotomy of the Latins, in that it could, and often does, mean the insertion of "the Christian religion minus European culture" into an "Asian culture minus non-Christian religion." This is inconceivable in the South Asian context just alluded to; what seems possible and even necessary there is not just *inculturation* but *"enreligionization"* of the church. I know that this way of putting it offends the Latin sensitivity. Even a knowledgeable and progressive theologian like Congar who, with his accustomed openness, made an honest effort to appreciate the theological frameworks of Indians like Amaladoss and Panikkar with their insistence on *Hindu Christianity* rather than Indian Christianity, did not hesitate to warn us of the "subtle and real danger" of syncretism and of the Christian faith being "contaminated" by a non-Christian religion.[6] These Indian theologians and their colleagues in the West are working with different paradigms!

Thirdly, the Greco-Roman model has bequeathed to the church what I have analyzed as the "instrumental theory" of inculturation taken for granted in Western theology.[7] Greek *philosophy* was pulled out of its own *religious* context and made to serve the Christian *religion* as a tool for doctrinal expression—that is, as *ancilla theologiae*, a medieval image used as early as Clement of Alexandria and expressed in its classic form in Peter Damien's allegorical interpretation of Deuteronomy 21:10ff.[8] In this scriptural passage, God ordains that an Israelite who sees a beautiful woman among his captured enemies could appropriate her as spouse so long as she would be of service. The conquest of another religion and the requisitioning of its beautiful philosophy to serve one's own religion constituted the basic policy that created the academic tradition in Western theology.

In the Asian context, this policy is unproductive, to say the least. To pluck a philosophy out of its soteriological context is to deprive it of its life. To employ a dead philosophy to construct a Christian doctrinal system is an intellectual feat that can at most satisfy only the person who indulges in that exercise. David Snellgrove's treatise on the "theology of the Buddhahood"[9] is a splendid illustration of what I am talking about.

If this Greek manner of "instrumentalizing" philosophy is unproductive in Asia, the Latin practice of "instrumentalizing" a non-Christian culture in the service of Christianity can be embarrassingly counterproductive, resulting as it does in a species of "theological vandalism" against which I warned Asian theologians several years ago.[10] This fear has already been confirmed by reports I have seen. Recently in Thailand, Buddhists have reacted with bitter indignation against the church for allegedly usurping their sacred symbols for Christian use! Inculturation of this type smacks of an irreverent disregard for the soteriological matrix of non-Christian religious symbolism, and it easily lends itself to the charge of being a disguised form of imperialism.

The fourth and final reason why the Greco-Roman model of inculturation succeeded in Europe but fails in Asia is that the historical circumstances surrounding the church in its early Mediterranean phase differ drastically from those of twentieth-century Asia. The Greco-Roman model was a viable and even a justifiable process of indigenization, given the socio-political context of those early centuries when the imperial religion of Rome was waning and Christianity was waxing. In fact, it was through inculturation that the church salvaged the culture of the Greeks and Romans from being buried in the archives of archeologists.

The exact converse is true in Asia. The imperial religion now in crisis is colonial Christianity, whereas so-called pagan religion is regaining vitality not only as a socio-political force that articulates the national ego of some of the decolonized countries but also as a current of contemporary spirituality that is passing through the length and breadth of the post-Christian West.

Placed against this background, inculturation-fever might appear to be a desperate last-moment bid to give an Asian facade to a church that fails to strike roots in Asian soil because no one dares to break the Greco-Roman pot in which it has been existing for four centuries like a stunted *bonsai*! No wonder non-Christians are as suspicious about the whole inculturation movement as some liberation theologians are skeptical about it.[11] In fact, one Buddhist, voicing the widespread reaction of his co-religionists, has questioned the good faith of the church in the following words:

> The so-called indigenization . . . appears to be a matter of tactics rather
> than one of appreciation and admiration of things indigenous. In other
> words it appears to be a camouflage resorted to with a view to breaking

down the apperceptive mass of Buddhists and to proselytizing them by using the vast financial resources of the church. It can be likened to the tactics of a chamelion which takes on the colour of the environment in order to deceive its prey.[12]

THE NORTH EUROPEAN MODEL OF CHRISTIANIZATION:
TOO LATE IN ASIA

If indeed the first centuries of Christianity do not point in a direction in which the church could be "at home" in Asia, then the early medieval experience seems to offer at least a useful analogy to *understand* the Asian context. But how far this third model is applicable in Asia today is quite another matter.

The terms of comparison are the North European *clannic* societies of the early Middle Ages, and the tribal societies still surviving in Asia. Their culture, in each case, can be described as basically religious, and their religiousness as essentially *cosmic*, a word I deliberately substitute for the term "animist" used by anthropologists. It is contrasted with the *metacosmic* religions that postulate the existence of a transphenomenal Reality immanently operative in the cosmos and soteriologically available within the human person either through agape (redeeming love) or through gnosis (redeeming knowledge). Such would be the Jewish and Christian faiths that are agapeic, and the monastic forms of Hinduism, Buddhism, and Taoism that are gnostic.

To extend further this comparison between the European prototype and the current Asian context, a very fundamental anthropological axiom has to be premised here—namely, that these two species of religion (cosmic and metacosmic) relate to each other as natural complements. In fact, a metacosmic religion (whether agapeic or gnostic) cannot be firmly rooted (that is, inculturated) in tribal societies except within the context of their cosmic religion; conversely, a cosmic religion is an open-ended spirituality that awaits a transcendental orientation from a metacosmic religion. It is therefore not a question of one replacing the other, but one completing the other in such a way as to form a bidimensional soteriology that maintains a healthy tension between the cosmic *now* and the metacosmic *beyond*.

Was this not the kind of inculturation that made Christianity "at home" not only in Northern Europe, but perhaps also in the South where the sap of cosmic religiousness was circulating beneath the veneer of Latino-Hellenic civilization? In fact, this is indirectly confirmed by Jean Delumeau's very persuasive thesis that both the Reformation and the Counter-Reformation were rigid conversion movements based on the belief that the rural masses of sixteenth-century Europe had not yet been fully weaned from their pre-Christian "paganism" (some going to the extent of thinking Italy to be as "pagan" as India!), so that the church's apprehensions about inculturation in Asia at that time, especially in the case of the Malabar and Chinese rites, could be partly explained by its inflexible stand against "paganism" at home![13]

We can, then, uphold the thesis that this early medieval form of inculturation makes sense in Asia wherever cosmic religion survives in its original format, undomesticated by any metacosmic religion. Today, however, very few pockets of such undomesticated areas are left in Asia, because these other religions have preceded Christianity by centuries and have already achieved in Asia that very kind of inculturation that Christianity accomplished with such success in Europe. The deva beliefs in South Asia, the Bon religion in Tibet, Nat worship in Burma, the Phi cult in Thailand, Laos, and Campuchea, Confucianism plus ancestor veneration in Vietnam, China, and Korea, the Kami worship of Shintoism in Japan are all cosmic religions that provided a very fertile soil for the great monastic religions to sink their roots deep into the Asian ethos. History shows, and sociology justifies, the phenomenon that one metacosmic religion already inculturated in a clannic society cannot be easily dislodged by another metacosmic religion except by protracted use of coercion—that is, by an *irreligious* resort to mass conversion.[14]

This means that in Asia Christianity has come on the scene a bit too late except perhaps in the Philippines and in some tribal societies of India and Southeast Asia where cosmic religions had remained intact. This third model of inculturation, therefore, is also obsolete in the greater part of Asia.

Thus, whoever thinks of inculturation not as an ecclesiastical expansion into non-Christian cultures but as the forging of an indigenous ecclesial identity from within the *soteriological* perspectives of Asian religions has begun moving in the right direction. Let me then indicate three road signs that have already helped us move further along this new path.

First, the bidimensional soteriology of non-Christian religions, wherein cosmic involvement with the present is tempered by a metacosmic orientation toward a future that constantly relativizes the here and now, offers a ready-made frame of reference for Christian spirituality, liturgy, ecclesial witness, social engagement, and theological formulations. Secondly, Asian theology is not the fruit of excogitation but a process of explicitation, or more specifically, a christic apocalypse of the non-Christian struggle for liberation. Thirdly, because we only explicitate a preexistent theology implicitly contained in non-Christian soteriologies, the procedure adopted is not one of "instrumentalizing" non-Christian schemas, but one of assimilation through participation in the non-Christian ethos, a baptism in the Jordan of our precursor's religiousness, a sort of *communicatio in sacris* that allows the "little flock of Christ" to feed freely on the Asian pastures that it has been trampling for centuries. There is no danger of theological vandalism here.[15]

Here I think it quite appropriate to cite the example of the Benedictine monk Swami Abhishiktananda (Henri le Saux) whose fair complexion and French accent were about the only things left of his European past after his baptismal immersion in the waters of Hinduism. He had so well absorbed Hindu spirituality (that is, theology in the primordial sense of God-experience) that his many utterances on the Christ-Mystery (theology in the secondary sense of God-talk) have become indispensable guideposts in the church's search for the Asian face of Christ.

THE MONASTIC PARADIGM: AN APPROXIMATION
TO THE ASIAN MENTALITY

The monastic tradition is precisely where the East is creatively silent in the West.

Here I take West and East not primarily as geographical divisions but as two human thrusts incomplete without each other and manifested phenomenologically in agapeic and gnostic idioms of the biblical and nonbiblical religions, respectively. Let me insist that even within Christian orthodoxy, which has always been agapeic, there was a legitimate line of gnosticism, whereas "heretical" gnoses "were only as it were the embroidery along the edge of this continuous line."[16] Similarly the gnostic religions, especially Hinduism and Buddhism, are not without their own versions of agapeic (*bhakti*) religiousness.

In the formative centuries of Christian monasticism the gnostic spirituality of non-Christians was gradually filtered into the agapeic religiousness of monks. While this symbiosis was taking place in the silence of monastic cells, academic theologians of the church were busy experimenting with the legal language of the Latins and the philosophical thought of the Greeks to make "precision instruments" that would enable the human mind to fathom the mystery of Christ, thus producing a vast corpus of theological literature that paved the way to christological dogmas and, centuries later, to an overgrowth of scholasticism.

If praxis is the first formulation of theory, then the monastic tradition conceals a theology that, if discovered, could redress the imbalance caused by academism.[17]

Thomas Merton did pioneering work in this direction and sharpened the church's monastic instinct blunted by centuries of neglect. He turned eastward, simply to rediscover the monk for the West. On the other hand, it was perhaps because monasticism was ignored by the academicians—and there were monks among them—that it was able to enjoy so much freedom. If the Western patriarchate can learn from its monastics to blend gnostic and the agapeic idioms, it would know how to appreciate the kind of "inculturation" Asia needs today.

Despite many temptations to the contrary, the Western monk and nun have learned that the (gnostic) ideal of *fuga mundi* ("flight from the world"—which influenced the early monastic interpretations of the call narratives in Matt. 19:21 and parallels, obviously in response to the contemporary demands of non-Christian asceticism) had to be complemented by an (agapeic) *involvement with the world's poor* who mediate Christ's presence for us. Thus true Christian renunciation of wealth was always considered to be made in favor of the poor so that from the anchoritic inceptions of the movement, as Lozano points out, the monks' search for God, at least in theory if not always in practice, was inseparably associated with their service to and solidarity with the poor.[18] When this balance between the gnostic and the agapeic components of spirituality was lost, as it often happened when concessions were made to mammon, God's rival and humanity's enemy, then obviously corruption set in, and monasticism became like salt without flavor, fit to be trampled upon.

By its failures, even more than its successes, Western monasticism has many lessons to teach the Asian church, for Asia is the oldest and the largest generator of *monasticism* besides being the inheritor of the largest portion of the world's *poverty*. Hence, the church is not competent to converse with Asia if it does not learn from its own Christian monastics the language of *gnosis* spoken by Asia's non-Christian monastics, and also the language of *agape*, the only one that the Asian poor can really understand. Asian monastics speak of the spiritual enlightenment that ensures the *interior liberation* of humans from their acquisitive instinct; but the Asian poor clamor for *social emancipation* from the oppressive structures into which this same acquisitive instinct is organized today. The monks and nuns point to the "metacosmic beyond" as the light that exposes the sinfulness of the "cosmic now," and the poor are not only the victims of this cosmic disorder but the agents of its imminent overthrow.

Whenever the *poverty voluntarily practiced* by Asian monastics is not directed positively toward the alleviation of the *poverty structurally imposed* on the Asian masses, then the resultant revolutions have adversely affected the feudalized monasteries of Asia, as for instance in Tibet and Mongolia. There, monastic poverty was not *socially* liberative. Hence, true inculturation is a rooting of the Asian church in the *liberative* dimension of voluntary poverty. When followers of Jesus opt to be poor for the sake of the gospel, they would live not only in solidarity with Asian monks and nuns in their quest for the metacosmic Reality, but more so in solidarity with the Asian poor who aspire for a *cosmic* order that is more just and holy.

A church inculturated in Asia is indeed a church liberated from mammon, and is therefore necessarily composed of the poor: poor by option and poor by circumstances. In other words, inculturation is the *ecclesiological* revolution already initiated by basic human communities, with Christian and non-Christian membership, wherein mysticism and militancy meet and merge: *mysticism* based on voluntary poverty and *militancy* pitched against forced poverty.

I can cite here at least four experiments made in Sri Lanka alone. (1) The most significant is the Devasarana, the monastery of the Anglican monk Yohan Devananda. His monastic presence in a Buddhist culture is made to coincide with his socialist involvement with peasant movements in rural areas. (2) The Satyodaya group, led by the Jesuit Paul Caspersz in Kandy, is an experiment of quite another kind; it is manifestly a sociological miracle, being a multiracial, multilinguistic, and multireligious community struggling hard to be a paradigm of a classless society in a country torn apart by ethnic conflicts. (3) The Christian Workers' Fellowship is perhaps the first such group to appear in the history of the Asian church. It has a Buddhist, Hindu, Christian, and

Marxist membership of both Sinhalese and Tamils; it operates in several places in Sri Lanka through basic *human* communities. (4) Fr. Michael Rodrigo, O.M.I., has established a community with similar aims at Buttala in the rural interior of Sri Lanka.

I am pleased that the Asian Monks' Congress, convened under the aegis of Thomas Merton in 1969, began discussing inculturation of monasticism in Asia. But it then stumbled over the scandal of Asian poverty in the second conference, held in 1973, and quite spontaneously came to realize in 1980, the third meeting of its kind, that monastic poverty is not Christian if it is not practiced in solidarity with Asia's poor.[19] The monastic instinct of the church, if sharpened by the gospel and not blunted by political naivety, cannot go wrong in Asia.

There is one special thing that Western monks or nuns can do for us, if they, like Merton, sensitize the Eastern part of their being. They can be interpreters for us to the Western patriarchate and defuse interecclesial tensions that invariably occur when we announce the good news *in our own tongues* to our own people (that is, the content of inculturation)—namely, that Jesus is the new covenant or the defense pact that God and the poor have made against mammon, their common enemy (that is, the content of liberation).[20] For liberation and inculturation are not two things anymore in Asia![21]

6

Speaking of the Son of God in Non-Christian Cultures

THE TWO CHRISTOLOGICAL PERSPECTIVES IN ASIA TODAY

The Fulfillment Approach

Any christological inquiry into Asian cultures will stumble against the fact that neither Jesus nor the religion he founded has won large-scale acceptance in Asia. Gautama the Buddha and Muhammad the Prophet are household names in the East, but Jesus the Christ is hardly invoked by the vast majority (over 97 percent) of Asians. Yet Jesus was no less an Asian than were the founders of Buddhism and Islam. Even of the few who believe in him, how many recall that God's Word had chosen to become Asian in wanting to be human? And how is it that the first Asians who heard him on our behalf and gave us the normative interpretations of his divine sonship made a significant breakthrough in the West but failed to penetrate the complex cultural ethos of Asia?

Asia's later disillusion with the "colonial Christ" no doubt added to this estrangement. But it also revealed that Christ could make sense in our cultures only to the extent that we use the soteriological idiom of "non-Christian" religions. I infer this from the fact that, when Jesus reentered the continent of his birth as the white colonizers' tribal god seeking ascendancy in the Asian pantheon, it was often the non-Christian religions that awakened the cultural ego of subdued nations in their collision with Christian powers, so that after four centuries of colonialism, Asia has surrendered only about two percent of its population to Christianity! If the Philippines went over to Christendom, it was because no other major Asian religion had struck institutional roots there earlier. The rapid rate of christianization in South America, contemporary Africa, and Oceania, in contrast to Asia's persistent defiance of the Christian kerygma, confirms my thesis: *the door once closed to Jesus in Asia is the only door that can take him in today—namely, the soteriological nucleus or the liberative core of various religions that have given shape and stability to our cultures.*

Written at the request of the editorial board of *Concilium* and first published in that journal, vol. 153 (1982), pp. 206-11.

I stress *soteriological* and *liberative*, for there is also a *sinful* and *enslaving* dimension to Asian religion. In a theological discourse such as this, therefore, one must discern the authentic core of an Asian religion from its perverted forms. It is the former that provides the indigenous idiom for meaningful Christ-talk in Asia. The failure to perceive this distinction accounts for the two christological perspectives prevailing today in the Asian church: a *Christ-against-religions* theology (of Western inspiration) and a *Christ-of-religions* theology.

The Christ-*against*-religions theology appeared in its crudest version when the colonial Christ came to redeem Asia's pagan soul from the grip of superstition through the medium of Western culture. Even De Nobili, Ricci, and others offered only a minor emendation to this "christology" in that they used "pagan" culture itself as their medium to draw Asians from their religions to that of Christ. But India's three-century search for the noncolonial Christ,[1] which included Hindu participation (see below), culminated in what is called "Indian christology"—actually a misnomer for a Christ-*of*-religions theology concerned with Hinduism.[2] This theology anticipated the fulfillment theory of the Lambeth Conference of 1930 and the Vatican Council of 1962: Christ works in all religions as the final consummation of all human search for redemption.

This theory, however, has already boomeranged on the Asian church. From Buddhists it hears that Jesus is only a bodhisattva (aspirant for enlightenment) whereas Gautama is *the* Buddha; from Muslims it hears that he is *a* prophet, even a special one, whereas Muhammad remains *the* prophet. Thus the Christian assertion that Jesus is *the* Son, *the* Christ, *the* Lord before whom other religious founders are mere prophets and precursors, is just one rival claim among others! Even Rahner's "anonymous Christianity" has been anticipated in Hinduism, which tends to gather other religions under its own salvific umbrella, neutralizing their uniqueness. According to a recent version of it, all religions are "alternate absolutes" with one undivided Goal, like the radii of a circle having but one center.[3] Hinduism, for the average Hindu, cannot but be the whole circle, though a Christian may hope to prove that Christ is its center! Buddhists have similarly appealed to their belief in the "solitary buddhas" (*Pacceka buddha*) to postulate the possibility of a non-Buddhist attaining nirvana outside institutional Buddhism but never outside the truth that the Buddha has discovered.[4]

The Contextual Approach

The fulfillment theory failed also in that it ignored the discomforting issue of *poverty*, which is as much a component of the Asian context as is religion. Besides, is not the story of Jesus preeminently the story of God-*with*-the-poor, God-*of*-the-poor, and God-*for*-the-poor? When this problem of poverty was reviewed, especially in the 1960s, the two christological perspectives were again in evidence. The neocolonialist school held that non-Christian religions were a positive hindrance to the humanizing task of eradicating poverty in Asia, a task that only Christianity, with its own (Western) model of "development," could achieve.[5] I even recall this task being described as "preevangelization," a prelude to Christ's arrival on the scene!

But a counterthesis was offered by the Christian ashrams where a contemplative adventure with God-in-Jesus was made to mirror Asia's own *religious* perception of *poverty*. According to the Eastern ascesis of detachment, *opted* poverty would be the redemptive antidote to acquisitiveness, the sin that generates *enforced* poverty. By giving a community orientation to those liberative values of Asian religion and poverty through common life and solidarity with its surroundings, the Christian ashram matured into a living christological formula in which Jesus was commemorated as "God-become-poor" and celebrated as the "divine guru" who offers interior liberation from greed and gathers the religious poor around himself into a saved and saving peoplehood: a replica of an inculturated church.

But was this ashramic Christ concerned about the colossal scandal of organized greed thriving on religious sanction? What about the sinful dimension of religion and poverty? Do inculturationists believe that voluntary poverty, when leavened by the liberative essence of Asian religion, could serve as a *prophetic* posture and a *political* strategy against enforced poverty, as it did in Gandhi's own case? I sympathize, therefore, with the Asian liberation theologians' insistence that the *God-Man* Jesus saves by being at once the *human* victim and the *divine* judge of Asia's institutionalized misery (Matt. 25:31ff.). They demand that authentic Christianity, which embodies this revolutionary activity of God's Son, be made to confront its own enslaving institutionalism.

But these liberation theologians are hardly ready to grant that Asian religions, too, have the kind of prophetico-political resources that a Christian minority must appropriate. For them, therefore, the encounter with Christ that they rightly see in Asia's struggle for full humanity implies a rejection of Asian religiosity in toto. Theirs is a theology of Christ-*against*-religions, which carries its colonialist and neocolonialist versions of the past into a crypto-colonialist finale, for it replaces "culture" and "development" of the previous eras with a "structural liberation" imported into Asia without first allowing Asia to liberate it of its restrictive notion of "religion." This notion is derived from three non-Asian sources: (1) Latin American liberationists' early unilateral rejection of religion as human alienation; (2) an unrevised nineteenth-century Marxian analysis of religion; and (3) Western biblical (e.g., Barthian) interpretation of religion(s) as antithetical to faith.

This conflict between the inculturationists' Christ-*of*-religions theology and the liberationists' Christ-*against*-religions theology erupted even as late as 1979 at the Third World Theologians' Asian Consultation.[6] When I proposed a polarity of "religion-poverty" as the context of Asian theology,[7] some theologians too hastily reduced religion to "inculturation" and poverty to "liberation"! Hence I repeat the plea I made during the subsequent controversy[8] to abandon the inculturation-liberation debate, because religion and poverty in their coalescence provide both the *cultural* context and the *liberationist* thrust required in any Asian christology. Besides, are they not the two perspectives along which Jesus himself revealed his divine sonship to his first Asian followers?

TWO PERSPECTIVES FOR A CHRISTOLOGY IN ASIA TODAY

Return to Jesus

Missiologists in the West have been disturbed by the news that some Asian theologians refuse to admit the "uniqueness of Christ." (Not only "Christ" but even the word "christology" are used here purely as conventional terms indispensable in an interecclesial theological discourse.) But the fact is that "Christ" (like "Son of God" or "Lord") is only a title, a human categorization by which one particular culture tried to "capture" the ineffable mystery of salvation communicated in the person and teaching of Jesus. What is absolute and unique is not the title, but what all major religions, some in theistic, others in nontheistic terms, have professed for centuries as the mystery of salvation manifesting itself at least in a trinal (if not trinitarian) form:

(1) Salvation as the *salvific "beyond"* becoming the human person's *salvific "within"* (e.g., Yahweh, Allah, Tao, Nirvāna, Tathatā, Brahman-Ātman),

(2) thanks to a *salvific mediation*, which is also revelatory in character (e.g., tao, *mārga, dharma, dabar,* image),

(3) and a (given) human *capacity for salvation* or a *saving power* paradoxically inherent in the human person (*puruṣa, citta, ātman,* etc.), despite being sheer "nothing," mere "dust," "soul-less" (*anātma*), a part of created "illusion" (*māyā*), immersed in this cosmic "vale of tears" (*saṃsara*) from which one yearns for perfect redemption.

Whether we should name this Theos-*Logos-Pneuma*, Father-Son-Spirit, or not name it at all, is not my immediate concern. Rather, I want to emphasize here that this "triune" mystery constitutes the basic soteriological datum in many of our religious cultures. The significance of speaking of the "Son of God" in such a context depends on the discovery of the *sensitive spot in the Asian heart* where Jesus, by making us retell his story, will find the proper idiom to communicate his unique identity within that tridimensional mystery. This sensitive spot can be discovered by retracing the steps that Jesus himself took in his effort to reveal his person in the Asian context of religion and poverty.

We know clearly that Jesus evolved his self-understanding and his self-revelation by his "baptismal immersion" into Asian reality. Let us concentrate on the two representative moments in this immersion: his first prophetic gesture at the Jordan and his last prophetic gesture on Calvary, both of which are designated in the Gospels as "baptism."[9] Jesus' self-effacing gesture at the

Jordan indicates a prior discernment concerning what was enslaving and what was liberative in the religion of Israel. The narrow ideology of the Zealots, the sectarian puritanism of the Essenes, the self-righteous legalism of the Pharisees, and the leisure-class mentality of the Sadducees had not impressed him. Rather, he opted for the *politically dangerous* brand of *prophetic asceticism* practiced by John the Baptizer. It was when he stepped into the Jordan to identify himself with the religious poor of the countryside and sought initiation under this great Asian guru, that he manifested his own salvific role to the people: the lamb/servant of God, the beloved Son (of God), the Word to be heard, the Giver of the Spirit, as the culture of the day phrased it. It was by entering into the soteriological nucleus of his culture that he revealed his salvific mission.

But Jordan was only the beginning of Calvary. The first baptism would soon lead to the other. Can there be an authentic religion without a painful participation in the conflicts of poverty? An Abba-experience without a struggle against Mammon? In fact, the money-polluted religiosity of his day conspired with the foreign colonial power—the inveterate alliance between religion and Mammon persisting to this day in Asia—to plant the cross where alone Jesus could reveal his true identity: "In truth this man was the Son of God" (Mark 15:39).

One thing is certain: if the revelatory and mediational dimension of the salvation-mystery (which has never ceased to shine like an unsetting sun on the soteriological horizon of Asia) is to manifest itself unambiguously for Asians in the human event of Jesus, then that event is, preeminently, the trajectory that *today* links the Jordan of Asian religion with the Calvary of Asian poverty. If this is done, the Asian cultures will open their repertoire of titles, symbols, and formulas to express their new discovery; the Asian church will sing not one but a thousand new canticles to its Spouse and Lord.

The New Asian Formula

The first meaningful christological formula—one that would be at once homologous and kerygmatic (that is, would make sense to Christians and non-Christians alike)—is an authentically Asian church. Such a church, however, is obviously a far cry from the esoteric community that it is today, ranting as it does in the occult language of colonial founders to be understood only by the initiated. To pull itself out of this incommunicado situation, the church must be given time to step into the baptismal waters of Asian religion and to pass through passion and death on the cross of Asian poverty. Until this *ecclesiological revolution* is complete, there will be no Asian christology. Instead, we shall have to be satisfied with mere "christological reflections" focused either on the problem of the "poor" (Kappan, Balasuriya) or on "religions" (Kadowaki, Abhishiktananda); or, as in the case of the extensive Indian hermeneusis of the fourth Gospel,[10] we shall rest content with the "political" standpoints and the "mystical" viewpoints of our theologians. But such efforts can only be the stirrings of a more radical desire to see Jesus' integral approach to asceti-

cism and politics, to religions and the poor, which will educe christologies from
the soteriological depths of our cultures.

Such a possibility is not remote. For the desired *ecclesiological revolution*
has already begun on the fringes of the church, where little laboratories of hope
(for the moment, few and far between) are struggling to be born. If they are on
the periphery of the mainline churches, it is because they have moved to the
very center of Asian reality. Their ambition to fuse politics with asceticism,
involvement with introspection, class analysis and self-analysis, the Marxist
laborare with the monastic *orare*, a militant repudiation of Mammon with a
mystic relationship with Abba their Father has plunged them into the liberative
streams of both religion and poverty. I hope that their *participation* ("baptismal immersion") in the twofold Asian reality will soon bloom into a spontaneous *explicitation* ("christic apocalypse") of the many hidden theologies issuing
out of the soteriological premises of Asian religions. That is how christologies
will be born in Asia. It is the story of Jesus retold by those Asian Christians
who have dared to traverse Jesus' own path from Jordan to Calvary.

Unquestionably this *participation-explication* approach to Asian christology ought to be complemented by a parallel search for that sensitive zone in the
Asian soul where Asia's own characteristic response to Jesus will be disclosed.
My suggestion is that non-Christian sages be encouraged to tell *their own* story
of Jesus. I am not referring to intellectuals and their "theory of religions,"
dismissed in the earlier part of this chapter. I speak rather of those *religious*
seekers who have opted to be *poor* in their search for the saving truth and who,
during their pilgrimage, encounter Jesus within their own soteriological perspectives.

This is not a dream, but a reality with a century and a half of history behind
it. From about 1820, many convinced Hindus have been grappling with the
mystery of Jesus. Whatever be one's reaction to their gnostic interpretations, in
them one can sense how Jesus makes his entry into a given Asian ethos. Some
of these Hindus might have acknowledged Jesus as savior (e.g., Subha Rao),
whereas many "followed him from a distance," like Peter (e.g., Raj Ram
Mohan Roy, Kesham Chandra).[11] Even trinitarian speculations were not absent
from their "christologies." But the fact that their interest in Jesus grew during
the Hindu renaissance deserves attention. As the Hindu self-consciousness was
awakened by the challenge of a politically extravagant Western Christianity,
some of these pilgrims of truth might have found in Jesus the "socio-political
texture of sanctity" they were looking for. Perhaps the aim of their search was
not an "ontological union" of God and humanity in the one person of Jesus,
but the "moral imperative" of reconciling *God-experience* with *human concern* in one identical salvific process. One understands why Gandhi looked
upon Jesus as a model *Sātyagrāhin*: "the suffering servant of Truth," if I may
coin a "christological title" that would describe the Gandhian Christ. Truth
(God) triumphs through suffering endured by Jesus. The Hindu doctrine of
renunciation allows the cross to shine as the supreme locus of Jesus' revelation
of the divine. What was a scandal to the Jews and folly to the Greeks could be

wisdom to a Hindu! In Asia today both interior freedom of soul and structural emancipation of the socio-political order (now ideologically polarized) demand a meaningful paradigm of *renunciation* (opted poverty) to justify the human struggle for total human liberation in terms of a salvific encounter with Ultimate Reality. One might legitimately ask whether Jesus' exaltation on the cross would not be that paradigm.

There are, of course, other "sensitive spots" in other areas wherein Jesus may find access to the Asian ethos under other names and titles, through other parables and paradigms. My surmise, therefore, is that a meaningful discourse on the "Son of God" will come about in Asian cultures mainly through an in-depth dialogue between *those* peripheral Christian communities and *these* non-Christian disciples of Christ trying to retell the story of Jesus to one another in terms of the one, absolute, triune mystery of salvation.

PART III

Theology of Liberation in Asia

7

Toward an Asian Theology
of Liberation

TOWARD A DEFINITION OF THE RELIGIO-CULTURAL
DIMENSION

Any discussion about Asian theology has to move between two poles: the *Third Worldness* of our continent and its peculiarly *Asian* character. More realistically and precisely, the common denominator linking Asia with the rest of the Third World is its overwhelming poverty. The specific character defining Asia within the other poor countries is its multifaceted religiousness. These two inseparable realities constitute in their interpenetration what might be designated as the *Asian context*, the matrix of any theology truly Asian.

We must immediately warn ourselves that Asian poverty cannot be reduced to purely "economic" categories, just as Asian religiousness cannot be defined merely in "cultural" terms. They are both interwoven culturally and economically to constitute the vast socio-political reality that is Asia. Hence an Asian theologian can hardly ignore Roy Preiswerk's appeal that the "dependency theories" of the Latin Americans (Cardos, Frank, Furtado, and others), which offer valid explanations of and useful strategies against the increasing poverty in the Third World, ought to be complemented (and I would add, even corrected) by the "cultural approach" of social scientists.[1]

This is nowhere more applicable than in Asia, for there is, in our cultural ethos, "a yet-undiscovered point" at which poverty and religiousness seem to coalesce in order to procreate the Asian character of this continent. In fact, history attests, as I shall indicate later, that the *theological* attempts to encounter Asian religions with no radical concern for Asia's poor and the *ideological* programs that presume to eradicate Asia's poverty with naive disregard for its religiousness, have both proved to be misdirected zeal. Hence the theologies now prevalent in the Asian church and the secular ideologies presently operating on this continent have all to be judged in the light of this axiom, as will be done in the course of this chapter.

Without, therefore, diluting or deemphasizing the economic features that define the "Third Worldness" of Asia, I shall concentrate on the "religio-

---

This was one of the three principal addresses at the Third Conference of the Ecumenical Association of Third World Theologians (EATWOT III) (Wennappuwa, Sri Lanka, 1979) which treated the theme of "Asia's Struggle for Full Humanity." The address stirred an intense debate between so-called theologians of inculturation and theologians of liberation. It first appeared in the Sri Lanka journal *Dialogue,* 6 (1979) 29-52.

cultural" dimension of the Asian context. As it might be objected that such a dimension exists also in all other poor countries, let me straightaway name three distinctive features that clearly demarcate the "religio-cultural" boundaries of Asia within the Third World: (a) linguistic heterogeneity, (b) the integration of cosmic and metacosmic elements in Asian religions, (c) the overwhelming presence of non-Christian soteriologies.

Linguistic Heterogeneity

Asia is diversified into at least seven major linguistic zones, the highest that any continent can boast of. There is, first of all, the Semitic zone concentrated in the western margin of Asia. The Ural-Altaic group is spread all over Asiatic Russia and northwest Asia. The Indo-Iranian stock and Dravidian ethnic groupings have their cultural habitat in southern Asia. The Sino-Tibetan region, by far the largest, extends from Central Asia to the Far East. The Malayo-Polynesian wing opens out to the southeast. Last but not least is the unparalleled Japanese, forming a self-contained linguistic unit in the northeastern tip of Asia.

The first theological implication of this linguistic heterogeneity derives from the very understanding of language. According to a nominalist view, a truth is apprehended intuitively and is *then* expressed outwardly through a language. If this were true, communal disturbances between linguistic groups—such as those in Sri Lanka or Cambodia or Burma—would have to be explained purely in terms of political and economic factors, which is not the case.

The fact is that each language is a distinctly different way of "experiencing" the truth, implying that linguistic pluralism is an index of religious, cultural, and socio-political diversity. Zaehner seems to be implying this when he, too, easily perhaps, typifies all Western religiousness as Semitic and Eastern religiousness as Indian.[2] I think it is only partially true to say that religion is an "experience" of reality, and language its "expression"; the converse is closer to the truth: *language is the "experience" of reality and religion is its "expression."* Religion begins with language. Would it be wrong to say that language is a *theologia incohativa*—an incipient theology?

What is the fundamental reality that a particular culture grasps through its own language and symbols? Read what the Asian proletariat has produced over the centuries, not merely the sophisticated writings such as the Vedas and Upanishads, the Tripitaka, the Torah, or the Tao Te Ching. Learn, first, the folk language. Assist at the rites and rituals of the Asian people; hear their songs; vibrate with their rhythms; keep step with their dance; taste their poems; grasp their myths; reach them through their legends. You will find that the language they speak puts them in touch with the basic truths that every religion grapples with, but each in a different way: the meaning and destiny of human existence; humanity's crippling limitations and its infinite capacity to break through them; liberation both human and cosmic; in short, the struggle for full humanness.

Every Asian culture has grown round a soteriological nucleus not yet assimilated into Christian consciousness. An Asian theology of liberation lies hidden there, waiting to be discovered by those ready to "sell all things." Recovery of an ancient revelation is indeed a new creation.

This means that the task of Asian theologians is more complex than that of their colleagues in the North Atlantic region and the Southern Hemisphere. After all, do not European theologians communicate in the same Indo-Germanic languages? Latin American liberation theologians think, act, and speak in a common Iberian idiom. They are all within reach of one another by means of a European medium of communication. Such is not the case in Asia.

It is therefore regrettable that Asians are not able to consult each other's hidden theologies except in a *non-Asian idiom*, thus *neutralizing the most promising feature in our methodology*. (The same applies to Africans.) We Asians professionally theologize in English, the language in which most of us think, read, and pray. The theological side of language in a "continent of languages" has been grossly underestimated and our stubborn refusal to consult each other's treasures directly in each other's linguistic idioms, or even to be familiar with one's own cultural heritage, will remain a major obstacle to the discovery of a truly Asian theology. This is not an appeal for chauvinism but a plea for authenticity imposed on us by what I have defined as the Asian context.

Integration of the Cosmic and the Metacosmic in Asian Religiousness

The institutional framework within which Asian religion operates is composed of two complementary elements: a cosmic religion functioning as the foundation, and a metacosmic soteriology constituting the main edifice.

By the term "cosmic religion" I wish to designate the species of religion that is found in Africa, Asia, and Oceania, and has been pejoratively referred to as "animism" by certain Western authors. Actually it represents the basic psychological posture that the *homo religiosus* (residing in each one of us) adopts subconsciously toward the mysteries of life—a sane attitude that an unwise use of technology can disturb. These mysteries relate to cosmic forces—heat, fire, winds and cyclones, earth and its quakes, oceans, rains, and floods—which we need and yet fear. Such forces serve as ambivalent symbols of our own subconscious powers, symbols freely employed in ordinary speech and in sacred rites, expressing our deepest yearnings. Even in the West, where these natural elements serve humanity through technology, can the Christian celebrate the paschal mystery without using fire and water? After all, if the theory of evolution is valid, we were all once a mountain, the crust of the earth, as well as water and fire, and all that we now carry with us as our material substratum, by which we become sacramentally present to others and to ourselves. We cannot be fully human without them.

In our cultures these natural elements and forces merge into the mysterious world of invisible powers that maintain the cosmic balance. They may appear in various guises in various regions: devas in the indianized cultures of Southeast Asia; Nats in Burma; Phis in Thailand, Laos, and Cambodia; Bons in

Tibet; Kamis in Japan; and of course, in the Confucianist worldview, departed ancestors belong to this invisible sphere. Rites, rituals, and a class of mediators form the constitutive elements of this religiousness.

A characteristic feature of Asian religiousness is that, unlike in Africa or Oceania, this cosmic religion does not appear in its pure and primordial form except in certain isolated pockets that anthropologists frequent. It has practically been domesticated and integrated into one or the other of the three metacosmic soteriologies—namely, Hinduism, Buddhism, and to some extent Taoism. The *summum bonum* (highest good) they present is a "transphenomenal beyond" to be realized here and now through gnosis. This justifies the existence of a certain spiritual elite—the sages, the wise—who become the personal embodiments of the mystico-monastic idealism held out as the climax of human perfection. They serve as models and symbols of "liberated" persons.

Hence these metacosmic soteriologies are never found in abstract "textual" form but always "contextualized" within the worldview of the cosmic religion of a given culture, creating a twofold level of religious experience, each level well integrated into the other. Here the Asian context differs from the African: due to this superimposition, non-African cosmic religions are not regarded as *salvific*. This is of great consequence for Asian theology. Let me mention in passing that it is invariably at the cosmic level that both technological and socio-political activity affect the major religions—a fact I shall discuss later.

(One might note, parenthetically, that the establishment of biblical religions, such as Islam in Indonesia and Catholicism in the Philippines, was easier partly because cosmic religions were found there in undomesticated or mildly domesticated forms at that time, whereas in Sri Lanka, India, Burma, and other countries, neither Islam nor Christianity could sweep over these cultures, because gnostic soteriologies had already domesticated cosmic religions into a well-integrated cultural system.)

Although these facts have hardly engaged the attention of Asian theologians, they have been a major preoccupation of anthropologists doing fieldwork in Asia.[3] The terms "cosmic" and "metacosmic" used here, however, have not been borrowed directly from anthropologists, but derive from a Buddhist self-understanding of the two levels: *Lokiya* (Sinhalese: *Laukika*) and *Lok'uttara* (Sinhalese: *Lokottara*). Buddhists recognize the two dimensions and explain their own religious experience in terms of this distinction (see Diagram 1).

My reference to Buddhism here is not accidental. To sharpen our focus on Asian religiosity, it is only reasonable that I should concentrate on one of the major religions. If my choice falls on Buddhism, it is not only because I am familiar with it, but even more because it is the one religion that is *pan-Asian* in cultural integration, numerical strength, geographical extension, and political maturity. Though an integral part of Indian heritage, now preserved in its Indian form only in Sri Lanka, it had penetrated practically every linguistic zone, even the Semitic, for a brief period.[4] In other words, Buddhism is not limited to one language or national group—as in the case of Hinduism and Taoism.

By allowing itself to be shaped by the various cosmic religions of Asia,

Buddhism has in turn molded several Asian cultures. Thus today there is an Asian Buddhist for every Catholic in the world. There are at least twenty political territories in Asia where Buddhism is either the official religion or a culturally influential factor. It is the one religion that can boast of Asia-wide ecumenical organizations such as the World Fellowship of Buddhists (WFB), the World Buddhist Sangha Council (WASC), and the World Buddhist Social Service (WBSS), all of which look to Sri Lanka for leadership. It is also politically the most resilient of Asian religions with a major role to play in the development and liberation of Asia, for it has a rich experience of Western colonialism, as well as of Marxism. Hence no Asian theology of liberation can be construed without consulting Asian Buddhism.

Diagram 1

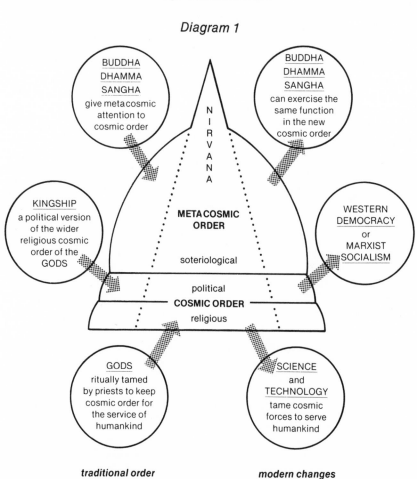

BUDDHA
DHAMMA
SANGHA
give metacosmic attention to cosmic order

BUDDHA
DHAMMA
SANGHA
can exercise the same function in the new cosmic order

N
I
R
V
A
N
A

KINGSHIP
a political version of the wider religious cosmic order of the GODS

METACOSMIC ORDER

WESTERN
DEMOCRACY
or
MARXIST
SOCIALISM

soteriological

political
COSMIC ORDER
religious

GODS
ritually tamed by priests to keep cosmic order for the service of humankind

SCIENCE
and
TECHNOLOGY
tame cosmic forces to serve humankind

traditional order   *modern changes*

Although Buddhism does not exhaust the whole phenomenon of Asian religiousness, it will nevertheless serve us as a paradigm to demonstrate how the interplay of the cosmic and the metacosmic levels of religious experience give a new point of departure for politico-social change and technocratic advancement in the very process of Asia's liberation—something that neither Western technocracy nor scientific socialism has sufficiently appreciated, and something that Asian theologies dare not underestimate.

The Overwhelming Presence of Non-Christian Soteriologies

Asia is the cradle of all the scriptural religions of the world, including Christianity, which, however, left Asia very early and forced its way back several centuries later as a stranger and "intruder" whom Asia consistently refused to entertain. Thus, after four centuries of missionary presence, Christians are numerically and qualitatively an insignificant minority: a mere 3 percent of the Asian masses. A good half of this Christian population is in the Philippines, which, in the process of becoming Christian, was forced to cut off its Asian roots. The Philippine church is only a magnified version of most Christian communities scattered in the Asian diaspora. Can a Christianity that has lost its "Asian sense" presume to create an Asian theology? Even the churches of the Oriental rites have frozen their early openness to the Asian reality.

This limitation, however, is also the greatest potentiality the Asian church has for creating a Third World theology that will radically differ from Latin American and African theologies. The liberation theologians of Latin America can speak of Christ and his liberation as a national and continental concern because of their traditional Christian heritage. This is why they are able to offer us a relevant Christian theology in place of the classic one of the European churches. So also will Africans soon become, numerically and qualitatively, a powerful Christian voice within the Third World. But Asia, as circumstances clearly indicate, will always remain a non-Christian continent.

This situation is ambivalent. It creates enormous opportunities for more creative modes of Christian presence in Asia by humble participation in the non-Christian experience of liberation; or it can repeat past mistakes in radically new ways. Let me substantiate this immediately by pointing out some salient features of non-Christian soteriology, using Buddhism as my basis and disclosing thereby the worldview within which the Asian church is called to make its options. If my approach is basically positive and appreciative, it is because I wish to absorb from these religions the Asian style of being, thinking, and doing.

NON-CHRISTIAN SOTERIOLOGY: SOME THEOLOGICAL PERSPECTIVES

I must, first of all, recapture the picture of institutional Buddhism with its cosmic and metacosmic dimensions of religious experience. To the cosmic sphere must be relegated (1) all socio-political activities and (2) technological and scientific progress; to the metacosmic pertains all that is ordained toward the interior liberation of the person. These elements are so well integrated that the equilibrium of the religious system could be disturbed by certain species of cosmic activities both political and scientific, as happens when Buddhism encounters Western capitalist technocracy or scientific socialism introduced by Marxists. To this I shall return below.

The sangha—the monastic nucleus round which Buddhism evolves—is the institutional center and the spiritual apex of a Buddhist society. It serves the cosmic level of human existence by directing its attention to the metacosmic goal, the ultimate Perfection (*Arahatta*) that consists in an absence of acquisitiveness and greed (*alobha*), absence of oppressiveness and hate (*adosa*), and perfect salvific knowledge (*amoha*). This is the classic description of nirvana. The monastic community that embodies this ideal is also a symbol of religious communism: they are called to share all things in common, "even the morsel of food falling into the begging bowl," as the Buddha has declared.[5]

The basis of such a community is poverty—voluntary renunciation of wealth and family life. But this poverty is sustained by the wealth-acquiring laity entrusted with the task of advancing material (technological) progress and socio-political well-being. The mutuality implied in this system of cosmic and metacosmic religion can best be discussed in terms of the bipolarity that exists between (1) wealth and poverty, (2) state and church, and (3) scientific knowledge and spiritual wisdom.

Wealth and Poverty

In this system they who renounce wealth are maintained by the wealth of those who do not. Wealth is at the service of poverty, and poverty is the condition for liberation from acquisitiveness and greed (*taṇhā, upādāna, lobha*). Hence all material progress is tempered by the ideal of nonacquisitiveness and sharing, of which monasticism is the symbol. This is, of course, the ideal; it is open to abuse, as history shows.

Hence, in an Asian situation, the antonym of "wealth" is not "poverty" but acquisitiveness or avarice, which makes wealth antireligious. The primary concern, therefore, is not eradication of poverty, but struggle against mammon—that undefinable force that organizes itself within every person and among persons to make material wealth antihuman, antireligious, and oppressive.

In fact, one source of Christian failure in Asia was its association with mammon (commercial and colonial exploitation) and its refusal to enter into the monastic spirit of non-Christian soteriologies. Today this mistake is repeated through massive "development" programs with which Asian churches (being minorities threatened by possible loss of identity) consolidate themselves into Western oases (big private educational, technological, or agricultural establishments run with foreign aid) thus forcing a non-Christian majority to depend on a Christian minority for material progress. This use of mammon, imposingly and manipulatively present in Asia, is a continuation, albeit in a new way, of the missiology of conquest and power characteristic of the colonial era. When a revolution rises against such establishments, the churches speak of themselves as being persecuted—when in reality they are only being trampled upon, like salt without flavor (Matt. 5:13).

On the other hand, mammon has not left monks in peace either. For a monk, poverty, not celibacy, is the most difficult virtue. The paradox of monastic renunciation is this: the holier the monk appears to be, the more generous his benefactors are toward him. The poorer he wants to be, the greater are the donations he receives. The more he runs away from riches, the closer he comes to it. The further he removes himself from society, the more crushing becomes its devotion to him. Thus, dependence on the people for material sustenance is at once the most basic condition and the most vulnerable feature of monastic poverty.

What is true of the individual monk is even more true of the monastery as a whole. Rich benefactors and even rulers show their appreciation by lavishing land and wealth on monasteries. Wealth-acquiring monasteries were not less frequently found in medieval Asia than in medieval Europe. In Tibet and Japan, at one time, armies were maintained to protect the wealth of monasteries.[6] In fact, the monastic ideal of religious poverty, which, by contrast, makes worldly happiness illusory, tends, under mammon's influence, to become a "worldly structure," which confirms Marx's opposite thesis that the abolition of such a religion as an "illusory happiness" is required for *real* happiness. In fact, it is here that Marxists and monks have collided in Asia.[7]

Theoretically, at least, Marxism is more consistently antimammon than purely antipoverty, in contrast with capitalist technocracy. In fact, no religious persecution under a Marxist regime can be compared to the subtle undermining of religious values that capitalist technocracy generates in our cultures. Marxism may purify institutional religion of its unholy alliances with the creators of poverty; capitalism pollutes religion by betraying it to Mammon. Hence, the monastic spirit, healthy in itself, has always required as its complement a state-machinery that could create a socio-political system conducive to its well-being. The reciprocity between religious and civil authority is an essential ingredient of the Buddhist worldview.

The State and the Sangha

Reciprocal dependence of the cosmic (*lokiya*) and the metacosmic (*lokuttara*) levels of existence is attested by the political history of Buddhist countries where the monastic institution has retained its spiritual status vis-à-vis political authority. This is especially true of southeastern Asia where state legitimization of the sangha is reciprocated by the monks' moral sanction of the state.[8] The relationship is, therefore, not purely spiritual but political as well, because in the Buddhist scheme of things, the metacosmic is founded on the cosmic. Buddhist monasticism is, therefore, never neutral to socio-political reality. This is why it has often suffered both persecution and purification in the hands of the state, but has also at other times initiated political revolutions against the state. In fact, one hears today of a military college in Thailand where monks prepare for an anti-Marxist war.[9] The anti-Christian and anticolonialist movements of Sri Lanka, Burma, and Indochina were born in Buddhist monasteries. There were several uprisings in China since the fifth century, stemming from messianic movements based on a desire for, here and now, the "era of justice and peace" foretold by the Buddha.[10] The dialectics between withdrawal from the world and involvement with the world—or contemplation and action—illustrative of the mutuality between the cosmic and the metacosmic, is nowhere so clearly attested as in the political role that spiritual persons play in a Buddhist culture.[11]

Let me illustrate this by referring to a lesson that Marxists learned about Buddhism.

As Holmes Welch has shown in his ponderous treatise on how Buddhism fared in revolutionary China,[12] Mao Tse Tung did not at first insist on the eradication of Buddhism or any other religion at the beginning of his rule. His thesis was that religion springs from certain socio-economic structures; when these structures would change, religion would automatically disappear. Instead of wasting time on eradicating a religion, he preferred to make use of it to change social structures, to expedite thus its own disappearance. This is the classic Marxist thesis.[13]

In this context we can understand the establishment of the Chinese-Buddhist Association (CBA) with its organ, *Modern Buddhism*. Through this periodical the CBA tried to convince Buddhists that they could live meaningfully within a Marxist regime by collaborating in the renewal of social structures. This is an understandable reaction. The CBA also organized goodwill missions to other Buddhist countries.

At the sixth session of the World Fellowship of Buddhists (WFB), the CBA tried to convince the Buddhist world that the Maoist vision of the new society was acceptable within the WFB. At this session, however, a right-wing ideology prevailed and the failure of the Chinese delegation became all too evident. The Tibetan issue, misconstrued by anticommunist Buddhists, dealt the CBA a setback. On the other hand, one can never underestimate the active part that the CBA played in the anti-Diem demonstrations in South Vietnam (1963–64), even though its success was only temporary. During the 1963–65 period, one was amazed at the debates conducted on mainland China about the "relevance of religions in the new society." Religion did not die with the change of structures; it only adapted itself and regained its vitality.

But by 1965 there were signs of a change in the Marxist thesis. Religion was described as a dying cobra that can strike before it dies. The need for killing it, therefore, was imperative. *Modern Buddhism* rather abruptly ceased to be published. The president of the CBA went out of circulation, and the Panchan Lama was demoted. These were the clouds that heralded the storm—the Cultural Revolution of 1966. There was a large-scale laicization of monks, not to speak of the destruction of statues and sacred articles. Since the persecutions of 644 and 845 A.D., Buddhism had never faced a worse crisis.[14]

The Soviet experience, on the other hand, moved in the opposite direction. It began with an intolerant attitude toward Buddhism and ended by dialoguing with it. The chief lama's attempts, at the beginning of the October Revolution, to accommodate Buddhist thinking and behavior to the new Marxist environment were not taken seriously by the Soviets. The Buddhists appealed to atheism and humanism as common ground they had with the Marxists, but at that time such overtures appeared naive to the new regime. Revolution was decidedly antireligious and anti-Buddhist. *Filosofikaya Entsiklopediya* (Moscow, 1960, vol. I) gives the classic Marxist explanation of Buddhism as ["opium"] pacifying the oppressed classes of Asia, making them submissive to oppressive regimes. One need not tarry here to determine how convinced the Marxists were of their position. The ruthless elimination of the lamas, persistently accused of spying for the Japanese, speaks for itself.

But in recent times we see a sudden change in the Soviet approach to Buddhism. One wonders what the reason might be. Is it simply an appreciation of the religious content of Buddhism or a recognition of the social reality of the Buddhist masses who did not give up their convictions? Or is it a recognition of the potentialities that Buddhism has for social change? Or might it be a search for political influence in Buddhist countries against Sino-American maneuvers?[15]

The first World Buddhist Conference since the Russian Revolution was held in Ulan Bator (Mongolia) in June 1970. Among the participants both Red China and Taiwan were conspicuously and significantly absent. The official statement issued by the organizers made it clear that their intention was to save Buddhist countries from American aggression.[16] There have been a number of follow-up efforts to this meeting.

Moreover, the *Bolshaiya-Sovetskaya Entsiklopediya* of 1971 (Moscow, vol. 4) seemed to take a more lenient stand in its entry on Buddhism and was clearly anti-Chinese in its evaluation of the Tibetan question, in contrast to the 1960 edition. This appreciation of Buddhism has been accounted for by Parfionovich, a Russian Marxist, who asks himself why Marxists should be so concerned about Buddhism. Should they rather not fight against Buddhism? His answer is enlightening:

> Well, didn't Lenin say that Marxism, far from repudiating the past, should absorb and work on it as the only sure foundation of a proletarian culture?
>
> Who can deny that Buddhism has been not simply a religion, but a way of life for millions? That its cultural and historical values have molded the spiritual heritage of mankind? Also, still conscious of Lenin's precept that we should absorb all the achievements of the human spirit, we are acutely aware that our knowledge of the ancient and medieval world is largely concerned with Europe and the Middle East. We know far too little of the great civilizations of Asia.[17]

Both the Chinese experiment, which moved from accommodation to persecution, and the Soviet experience, which started with intolerance and ended up with dialogue, show that Buddhism is a power to be reckoned with. This power is not merely in the sacred texts of a bygone era but in the culture of peoples who have learned to integrate their cosmic concerns with a metacosmic vision—politics with spirituality.

Scientific Knowledge and Spiritual Wisdom

Technology tames cosmic forces and puts them at the service of humanity. The religious rites by which such powers were tamed in an earlier age may recede to insignificance as technology advances. There is, in a way, a desacralizing process, which could be interpreted as a liberation of humanity from superstition. But this is not all there is to it.

Technology is as ambivalent as the cosmic forces it claims to domesticate. Its unwise use, far from making cosmic forces really submissive to humanity, has only provoked them to retaliate and enslave humans with pollution, consumerism, secularism, materialism, and a host of evils that a technocratic society has produced in the First World. Besides, it has deprived the human mind of myth and ritual, two things by which humanity enacts its deep yearnings and keeps itself sane in mind and body. Can technology liberate the person? Certainly not in the form in which "Christian" nations have offered it to us. It takes away cosmic religion from the masses, and replaces it with neurosis. It takes away religious poverty only to give us mammon instead.

One is annoyingly amused, therefore, to read the theological justification of this development ideology in the classical thesis put forward by Van Leeuwen: the scientific and industrial revolution, with its modern secular culture, is to be welcomed as the fruit of (Western) Christianity; hence Christianity should carry this mission to Asia and *liberate* its masses from superstitious religiosity! The implication of this thesis seems to be that the church's mission is to use Western ideology and theology to eradicate at once the religiosity and the poverty of our continent! Ninian Smart of Lancaster University has described this missiology beautifully when he called it "western Tribalism."[18]

It took a wise man in the West—Paul VI—to appeal for reciprocation between the technician busy with scientific progress and the wise person who could guide the technician from a contemplative distance.[19] Thus, the patriarch of the Western church has recognized the need for a bipolarity between secular knowledge and spiritual wisdom. Asia has taught this for centuries in its religious view of material progress.

Look at the ancient irrigation works of Sri Lanka. What a feat of engineering! How, then, has our technology failed to keep pace with the West? After all, was not technology—or *ars mechanica* as the medieval Europeans called it—imported from the East after the Crusades?[20] Why are the skills of the past still hiding behind the facade of archeological remains? One thing is sure. The technician in our culture remained an illiterate artisan whose skills did not enter the ola-leaf manuscripts that the monks authored. The literati, who knew the arts, perpetuated what they knew; cosmic or natural sciences did not enter their domain. Thus, technology, once begun, seems to have disappeared in the course of time. This could very well be a fundamental weakness in the Asian system.

But there is another side to it. In that system, scientists could not create a class of white-robed clerics to officiate in the sanctum of the laboratory, preaching a dangerous brand of "neognosticism" claiming that the power to liberate humanity resides in the scientific knowledge of nature's secrets.[21] The Buddhist worldview has always preserved the orientation that Paul VI advocated: true gnosis is spiritual wisdom guiding scientific knowledge to the fullness of authentic development.[22] Technology is an induced cosmic process, which is at once a conscious continuation of biological evolution, and which, like it, becomes humanized only by a metacosmic orientation. The thesis that superstition has to be removed by technology must also be qualified by the fact that the cosmic religions in Asia are already being purified by the metacosmic orientation they receive in the hands of monastic religions—a fact that my own fieldwork has amply demonstrated, but which I cannot detail here.[23]

The priest and journalist Piero Gheddo is also oversimplifying the case when he says that Western progress came from the Christian doctrine of the "dignity of man" [*sic*] and that underdevelopment among us Asians is partially explained by a lack of such a perspective in our cultures.[24] Taking a contrary viewpoint, a distinguished economist has seen in our "slow progress" a certain wisdom that in the long run preserves human dignity. He called it "Buddhist economics" and epitomized it in a now popular slogan: "Small is beautiful"[25]—which means, "mammon is ugly."

"Freedom from poverty," the goal of Western technocracy, can be an enslaving pursuit ending up in hedonism if not tempered by the "freedom that comes from poverty." This is not a glorification of poverty, the "spirituality" that exploiters usually impose on the poor. I refer rather to the "religious" understanding of poverty, which sets the church before the choice of either Marxist materialism or the hedonism of affluent societies! If "it is to the former that the church turns its attention since it is potentially more renewing, closer to the call of justice and equality, even if to a lesser degree, a defender of formal liberties,"[26] it is equally true that Marxism has not appreciated fully the religious dimension that Asian cultures attribute to poverty. Latin American liberation theology, the *only* valid model of theology for the Third World today, also lacks a perceptive understanding of this monastic ideal. The Marxist embarrassment in the face of Asia's indestructible religiosity, as described above, may reappear in an Asian theopraxis too heavily dependent on the Latin American model.

The Asian religious attitude to poverty, even in the context of its march to economic progress, differs from the Latin American attitude as a *psychological* method differs from a *sociological* one. In the former, voluntary poverty is a spiritual antidote; in the latter it is a political strategy (see below). Mammon—which some Christian theologians have translated with the word "capital"[27]—needs to be vehemently opposed with both methods. To borrow Maoist jargon, a structural revolution can avoid much of its unnecessary violence if accompanied (not followed) by a cultural revolution. A "liberation-theopraxis" in Asia that uses only the Marxist tools of social analysis will remain un-Asian and ineffective. It must integrate the psychological tools of introspection that our sages have discovered. A new society evolves with the evolution of the New Person, and vice versa.

May I suggest a useful exercise that might illustrate what I am trying to say? Read theologically the revolutionary theory and praxis of Che Guevara in the light of a similar reading of Ho Chi Minh. Taste the distinctly Christian flavor in the former. Then note the difference in the latter. What you notice would be the *Asian sense.*

THE ASIAN SENSE IN THEOLOGY

To predispose ourselves to receive the *Asian sense* into our Christian consciousness, certain inhibitions inherited from the local churches of the West first need to be eliminated. Consistent with the methodology used so far in this chapter, the following review of our theological past will be made from (1) the *Third World point of view* in general, and from (2) the *Asian point of view* in particular. The contents of Asian theology do not concern me here. All I hope to achieve by this critique is to discover the *Asian style of doing theology.*

A Third World Critique of Our Theological Past

In the course of this discussion we have considered two "secular" movements engaged in liberating us from our "poverty"; both originated in the West. The first is Marxist socialism and the other is the developmental ideology associated with capitalist technocracy. The West is also spiritually present through the church, which, for the most part, is an extension of Western Christianity. Thus, the church too reflects in its own theological self-understanding the ideological conflicts of the West. Hence, this inquiry into the theological equipment of the church.

The Asian church, for the moment, has no theology of its own, though the cultures that host it teem with theology. The church is caught today between two theologies, which are as Western as the secular ideologies just mentioned. The first is the classic European theology, which, in its various brands, is officially taught in all major institutions of the Asian church. The second is the Latin American liberation theology, which is also making itself felt in certain theological circles. These theologies, of course, are diametrically opposed to each other, as are also the secular ideologies mentioned above.

Classic theology in the West, which has gone through the mill of renewal since the nineteenth century, is said to have made a major "breakthrough" in the middle of this century, climaxing in modern theology with its openness to the world. According to Mark Schoof, the chief centers of this renewal were the French and German linguistic zones, because, in his words, "it was there that the theologians seemed to have the necessary scientific tradition and sufficient creative energy at their disposal."[28] According to the same author, one major source of inspiration for Catholic renewal of European theology can be traced back to Protestantism in Germany.[29]

Schoof summarizes his understanding of this period of European theology in the title of his thesis: "Breakthrough." But an Asian looking from a critical distance sees quite another picture. The real breakthrough in Western theology came with the Latin American critique of the same scientific tradition that Schoof proudly refers to. The openness to the world that European theologians achieved up to the 1960s by dialoguing with contemporary philosophies[30] is only a mild reform compared with the achievements of Latin Americans from the 1960s onward. The liberationists effected a complete reversal of method. They seem to have done to European theology what Feuerbach did to Hegelian dialectics. They put theology back on its feet. They grounded it on theopraxis. What was formerly revolving around a Kantian orbit was made to rotate around a Marxian axis.[31]

For us Asians, then, liberation theology is thoroughly Western, and yet so radically renewed by the challenges of the Third World that it has a relevance for Asia that classic theology does not have. The Ecumenical Association of Third World Theologians (EATWOT) is perhaps the first tangible fruit in Asia of this encounter with liberation theology. In the churches of the East this new method has already begun to compete with the traditional theology. What the Latin Americans claim, and what we Asians must readily grant, is that it is not perhaps a new theology, but a new theological method, indeed the correct method of doing theology.

The features of this methodology peculiarly relevant for us in Asia are contained in Jon Sobrino's lucid comparison of European and Latin American theologies.[32] The first feature is that the Kantian attempt to liberate reason from authority paved the way for a theological preoccupation with harmonizing faith with reason, whereas the Marxian attempt to free reality from oppression did not receive theological attention in Europe until the Latin Americans made an issue of it.[33] Thus the use of philosophy to rationally explain away suffering or to define God and the divine nature in such a way as to justify the existence of oppression and injustice was understandable in a European socio-political context. But the replacement of philosophical speculation with sociological analysis in order to change rather than explain the world of injustice has become the immediate concern of liberation theology. Such a concern cannot come within the scientific purview of European theology, whether Protestant[34] or Catholic.[35]

The second feature, quite important for Asians, is the primacy of praxis over theory. Spirituality, for instance, is not the practical conclusion of theology but the radical involvement with the poor and the oppressed, and is what creates theology. We know Jesus the *truth* by following Jesus the *way*.

Thirdly, this way is the way of the cross, the basis of all knowledge. Thus, the growth of the world into God's kingdom is *not* a progressive development, but a process punctuated by radical contradictions, violent transformations, and death-resurrection experiences—what Sobrino calls the *ruptura epistemologica*—scripturally founded in the "transcendence of the crucified God."[36]

Fourthly, we see that it is not a "development theology" such as would justify and perpetuate the values of an acquisitive culture, but a "liberation theology" demanding an asceticism of renunciation and a voluntary poverty that rejects acquisitiveness. This resultant spirituality is not self-enclosed, for it is motivated by the desire to bring about the kingdom of God here on earth. What it inculcates is not merely a passive solidarity with the poor in their poverty and oppression, but also a dynamic participation in their struggle for full humanity—indeed, a dynamic following of Christ![37]

Finally, the encounter of God and humanity—that is, the interplay of grace and liberty—is seen as the obligation to use all human potentialities to anticipate the kingdom, which nevertheless remains God's gratuitous gift. This explains the liberationist's political option for socialism—that is, for a definite social order in which oppressive structures are changed radically, even violently, in order to allow every person to be fully human, the assumption being that no one is liberated unless everyone is.

Both this Latin American liberation theology and its European predecessor receive their contextual significance in Asia precisely in relationship to the aforesaid Western ideologies with which they are very closely connected. My earlier criticism of how these ideologies operate in Asia has clearly situated the two theologies, too, in the context of Eastern religion. Hence the need to complement the Latin American method with an Asian critique of classic theology.

The Asian Style as Asian Theology

Beijing has taken a stand on the future of Buddhism: "The Communists hold that, as a *religion*, Buddhism will gradually die out, as history moves forward; but as a *philosophy* it merits careful study."[38]

This sort of apocalyptic optimism, which turns hopes into predictions, is not new in the history of Asian Buddhism. Christian missionaries in Sri Lanka used to pronounce such prophecies in the last century[39] when the whole colonial state machinery was backing their missions against the Buddhists.[40] Buddhism, however, has lived to tell the tale. The analogy with the Chinese situation need not be labored here.

Marxists maintain that it is *religion* that will die, but not *philosophy*, which merits study. Here again I cannot help drawing a parallel with theologians of the West who also have detached religion from philosophy in their theology of religions. In fact, the inherent incapacity of both classic Marxism and classic theology to grasp the Asian sense as revealed in the multifaceted religiousness of our peoples is ultimately rooted in this unhappy dichotomy both have inherited from a tradition that began perhaps with the early Western encounters with non-Christian cultures.[41]

Let me, then, put things back in focus. In all the nonbiblical soteriologies of

Asia, *religion* and *philosophy* are inseparably interfused. Philosophy is a religious vision; religion is a lived philosophy. Every metacosmic soteriology is at once a *darsana* and a *pratipada*, to use Indian terms—that is, an interpenetration of a "view" of life and a "way" of life. In fact, the oft-repeated question, whether Buddhism is a philosophy or a religion, was first formulated in the West, before it reached Beijing via Marxism. For in the Buddha's formula, the fourfold salvific truth incorporates the path as one of its constituents, and the eightfold path coincides with the realization of the truth.

Here let me refer to the current trend of using "Buddhist techniques" of meditation in "Christian prayer" without any reverence for the soteriological context of such techniques. Such a trend is based on the naive presupposition that the (Buddhist) way could be had without the (Buddhist) truth. It is time to impress on our theologians that in our Asian culture method cannot be severed from goal. The word "technique"—now misused in task-oriented cultures to mean a mechanical action that, when done according to set rules, produces predictable results—must be traced back to its original Greek sense. *Techne* is not a mechanical action, but a skill, an art; in Asian traditions, the art of doing a thing is itself the thing done. The perfection to be achieved is the style of achieving it! The obvious corollary is that the Asian method of doing theology is itself Asian theology. Theopraxis is already the formulation of theology.

Thus the mutuality of praxis and theory that defines the Asian sense in theology is the missing ingredient in the theology of religions, which its practitioners have uncritically accepted and which hampers their task of acquiring the Asian style.

This inadequacy seems to have been introduced by the early fathers of the church who, in their dialogue with nonbiblical systems, restricted their interest to the philosophical rather than the religious plane. They further impressed this dichotomy on the Western theological tradition when they took "pagan" philosophy out of its religious context and turned it into an intellectual weapon serving Christian apologetics against those very religions! Thus philosophy became the handmaid of Christian religion, *ancilla theologiae*, as already noticed in the writings of Clement of Alexandria and Peter Damien.[42] It is in this play of circumstances that one can understand the two permanent blights that Western theology of religions received early on in its history.

First, the use of philosophy minus religion imparted a *cerebral thrust* to the theology of religions. This emerged side by side with an abhorrence of pagan religious practices—an old Semitic intransigence continuing up to the Apostolic era. Nevertheless, in the course of time these religious practices did influence Christian liturgy and ethics, even though theology held fast to its *ancilla*! Thus from the very beginning, theology and theopraxis parted ways. The God-talk of theologians and the God-experience of monastics ran parallel but never really touched. The former was working on "pagan" thought and the latter on "pagan" spirituality! The academicians and the mystics lived in mutual suspicion.

The second blight is even deeper. It is the apological technique of using a non-Christian religion against itself. This later became a missiological strategy, still resorted to in the theology of religions. It began with the way a pagan philosophy was removed from its original religious context and made to serve Christianity, enabling the Christian religion not merely to enrich itself with new intellectual equipment but also to counteract pagan religions. This process of instrumentalization is not absent even in De Nobili and Ricci, the missionary innovators of seventeenth-century Asia. What the early fathers did to nonbiblical philosophy, later Christians did to Asian *culture*. They truncated it from its religious context and turned it into a means of conversion. It was a step forward, no doubt, but in the same direction! To this category must be relegated also the Christian guru who, as mentioned earlier, plucks Zen and Yoga from the religious stems that give them sap, and adorns Christian spirituality with sapless twigs!

This species of theological vandalism has been euphemistically expressed by a new Christian use of the word "baptism." One hears of baptizing Asian cultures, and now after Vatican II, baptizing Asian religiousness. In its scriptural usage, baptism expressed the most self-effacing act of Christ, first in the Jordan where he knelt before his precursor (Mark 1:9–11), and then on the cross (Mark 10:35–40; Luke 12:50) where, as the suffering servant, he ended his earthly mission in apparent failure. But now the word has come to mean Christian triumphalism, which turns everything it touches to its own advantage, with no reverence for the wholeness of the religious experience of others.

CONCLUSIONS

1. Asian theology is our way of sensing and doing things as revealed in our people's *struggles for spiritual and social emancipation*, and expressed in the idioms and languages of the cultures such struggles have created.

2. Theology, then, is not mere God-talk, for in our cultures God-talk *in itself* is sheer "nonsense." As evidenced by the Buddha's refusal to talk of nirvana, all words have *silence* as their source and destiny! God-talk is made relative to God-experience. The word game about nature and person or the mathematics of one and three have only generated centuries of verbosity. It is wordlessness that gives every word its meaning.

This inner *harmony* between *word* and *silence* is the test of Asian authenticity, indeed it is the Spirit, the Eternal Energy that makes every word spring from Silence and lead to Silence, every engagement spring from renunciation, every struggle spring from a profound restfulness, every freedom spring from stern discipline, every action spring from stillness, every development spring from detachment, and every acquisition spring from nonaddiction. Because silence is the *word unspoken* and the word is *silence heard*, their "relationship" is not one of temporal priority but of dialectical mutuality. It is the Spirit of Buddhist wisdom and Christian love. If there is harmony between our speech and our silence, whether in worship or service or conversation, the Spirit is among us.

3. The same *harmony* reigns between *God-experience*, which is silence, and the *concern for humanity*, which makes it heard. One is not temporally prior to the other. It is, rather, the mutuality between wisdom and love, gnosis and agape, *pleroma* and *kenosis*, or as the Buddhists have put it, between "knowledge that directs us to nirvana and the compassion that pins us down to the world."[43] For liberation-praxis is at once a withdrawal into the metacosmic and an immersion into the cosmic.

4. The most subtle point of this dialectic is between authority and freedom. The magisterial role in the Asian church has to be earned by the Master's competence to mediate liberation. Authority makes no external claims. Authority is competence to communicate freedom. Those who lack competence use power. "With whose authority?" asked the power-thirsty clerics from the Son of Man who submitted himself to that very power in order to vindicate his authority. His authority was his freedom available to all who touched him. It is a self-authentication derived from a liberation-praxis; it is a concern-for-humanity testifying to a God-experience; the two prongs of a liberation struggle.

5. To regain its lost authority, therefore, the Asian church must abdicate its alliances with power. It must be humble enough to be baptized in the Jordan of Asian religion and bold enough to be baptized on the cross of Asian poverty. Does not the fear of losing its identity make it lean on mammon? Does not its refusal to die keep it from living? The theology of power-domination and instrumentalization must give way to a theology of humility, immersion, and participation.

6. Hence, our desperate search for the Asian face of Christ can find fulfillment only if we participate in Asia's own search for it in the unfathomable abyss where religion and poverty seem to have the same common source: God, who has declared mammon to be the enemy (Matt. 6:24).

7. What, then, is the locus of this praxis? Certainly not the "Christian life lived within the church in the presence of non-Christians"; rather, it is the God-experience (which is the other side of the concern-for-humanity) of God's own people living beyond the church. It is among non-Christians that the church is called to lose itself in total participation. That is to say, *theology in Asia is the Christic apocalypse of the non-Christian experiences of liberation.*

8

The Place of Non-Christian Religions and Cultures in the Evolution of Third World Theology

THEOLOGY OF RELIGIONS: CURRENT BOUNDARIES OF ORTHODOXY

Basis and Background: The Third World as a Theological Perspective

The term "Third World" is a theological neologism for God's own people. It stands for the starving sons and daughters of Jacob—of all places and all times—who go in search of bread to a rich country, only to become its slaves. In other words, the Third World is not merely the story of the South in relation to the North or of the East in relation to the West. It is something that happens wherever and whenever socio-economic dependence in terms of race, class, or sex generates political and cultural slavery, fermenting thereby a new peoplehood. Because, however, there is no people unless summoned by God, and no God worth talking about except the God who speaks through a people, all theology is about a people's God—that is, about God's people. The major focus of all "God-talk" or theology, then, must be the Third World's irruption as a new peoplehood announcing the liberating presence of a God who claims to humanize this cruel world.

But the irruption of the Third World is also the irruption of the non-Christian world. The vast majority of God's poor perceive their ultimate concern and symbolize their struggle for liberation in the idiom of non-Christian religions and cultures. Therefore, a theology that does not speak to or speak through this non-Christian peoplehood is an esoteric luxury of a Christian minority. Hence, we need a theology of religions that will expand the existing boundaries of orthodoxy as we enter into the liberative streams of other religions and cultures.

One regrets, therefore, that the only Third World theology presently being given substance is circumscribed by the exclusively Latin and Christian context of its origin. This remark is not leveled against the Latin American model but

---

One of the three principal addresses at the Fifth Conference of the Ecumenical Association of Third World Theologians (EATWOT V) in New Delhi, 1981 which examined the theme "The Irruption of the Third World: Challenge to Theology." First published in the *CTC Bulletin* (Singapore), 3 (1982) 43-61.

against the antithetical attitudes it has evoked in the Afro-Asian churches, in that some "liberationists" want to duplicate a Latin, Christian model in their non-Latin and non-Christian environments, thus driving "inculturationists" to a defensive extreme.

In fact, at the EATWOT Asian consultation in 1979,[1] I tried to forestall this futile debate by avoiding the liberation/inculturation schema and by defining theology as a discovery rather than an invention—that is, as a Christian participation in and a christic explicitation of all that happens at the deepest zone of a concrete ethos where religiousness and poverty, each in its liberative dimension, coalesce to forge a common front against mammon.[2] Nevertheless, the subsequent controversy fell back upon the old paradigm and reduced religion and poverty to the categories of inculturation and liberation, respectively,[3] though efforts were made to restore the original framework in which the *cultural* context of theology was equated with the *liberative* dimension of religiousness and poverty.[4]

The polarization continues to this day. The reason, presumably, is that in both the First and the Third Worlds there still lurks a crypto-colonialist theology of religions (and cultures) that keeps our revolutionary rhetoric from resonating in the hearts of the Third World's non-Christian majority. This is an issue that demands frank and open discussion in all the churches.

My analysis of this question presumes that every religion, Christianity included, is at once a sign and countersign of the kingdom of God; that the revolutionary impetus launching a religion into existence is both fettered and fostered by the need for an ideological formulation; that its institutionalization both constrains and conserves its liberative force; that religion, therefore, is a potential means of either emancipation or enslavement.

But, theologically speaking—which is to say, "from a Third World perspective"—the test case that reveals the twin aspect of sin and grace in religion is its response to the phenomenon of poverty. Poverty is itself ambivalent. It can mean dispossession forced upon the masses by the hedonism and acquisitiveness of the greedy. But it can also mean the virtue of poverty, which, according to Albert Tevoedjre's thesis, is "the status of someone having what is necessary and not the surplus," a conditio sine qua non for the elimination of what I have defined here as enforced poverty.[5]

I grant that this criterion is not universally accepted, nor is the ambivalence of the religious phenomenon comprehensively spelled out in theological circles. Thus, a certain unilateral view of religions still prevails and accounts for the polarization of the church into a Christ-*against*-religions theology and a Christ-*of*-religions theology. The rift between liberationists and inculturationists is only a recent manifestation of this polarization; there have been other versions earlier, as indicated in Diagram 2.

The Liberation Thesis on Religion: Its Western and Colonialist Character

The contrast between these two perspectives (Christ-*against*-religions and Christ-*of*-religions) is quite evident even among Latin American theologies.

Diagram 2

CHRIST AND RELIGIONS

Historical Panorama of a Polarization

Christ-AGAINST-Religions	Christ-OF-Religions
SIXTEENTH CENTURY ONWARD The **COLONIALIST CHRIST** of early Western missionaries conquers non-Christian religions, which are linked with the **moral poverty** of "colonized" nations.	**NINETEENTH CENTURY ONWARD** The **GNOSTIC CHRIST** of Indian theologians; beginning of the fulfillment theory of religions.
The medium of his action is the **Western** form of **civilization**.	The link between religion and material poverty is ignored.
LATE 1960s The **NEO-COLONIALIST CHRIST** of the developmentalists conquers non-Christian religions, which are linked with the **material poverty** of "developing" nations.	**LATE 1960s** The **ASHRAMIC CHRIST** of monks and mystics, incarnated through traditional practice of religious poverty —i.e., voluntary acceptance of material poverty (Renunciation, monasticism).
The medium of his action is the **Western** model of **development**.	The link between religion and structural poverty is ignored.
LATE 1970s The **CRYPTO-COLONIALIST CHRIST** of the liberationists conquers non-Christian religions, which are linked with the **structural poverty** of Third World nations.	**LATE 1970s** The **UNIVERSAL CHRIST** of the inculturationists, particularized in cultures through the appropriation of religious structures (idioms, symbols, moods, etc.).
The medium of his action is the **structural liberation** based on Marxist occidentalism and **Western Biblicism**.	The link between religion and liberation struggles is ignored.

put Christ against *religion as such* (phase 3). In this lies both the continuity and the contrast between early and modern versions of this conservative evangelism!

The narrow concept of religion as advocated by the liberationists seems more Greek than Roman. Most Greek apologists were inclined to churn "paganism" theologically and extract only its philosophy, leaving aside its religion as incompatible with Christianity. The tendency to squeeze religion out of human existence (by way of sacralization and secularization, which are two sides of the same coin) is not alien to Western tradition. Schillebeeckx has cogently argued that even the modern phenomenon of secularization took form under the sacred shadow of medieval cathedrals.[13]

But the two forms in which this tendency influenced liberationist interpretation of religion appeared only within the last hundred years. For the philosophical rejection of (the Christian) religion characteristic of certain intellectual movements in Europe (Enlightenment, scientific revolution, rationalism) found an ideological as well as theological formulation in the two Karls of "dialectical" fame. Marx's dialectical materialism set religion against *revolution*; Barth's dialectical theology opposed it to *revelation*. In their systems, religion was a major obstacle to liberation and salvation, respectively.

In dismissing the immanentist thesis coming down from Schleiermacher to Otto, a thesis that postulated a "religious a priori" in the human person, Barth initiated an evangelistic theology that reduced the notion of religion to a blasphemous manipulation of God, or at least an attempt at it. The pioneering Protestant exegetical tradition—anterior to and stimulative of later Catholic biblical scholarship—was seriously infected by this bias. Kittel, for instance, referring to the conspicuous infrequency of such words as *threskeia*, *deisidaimonia*, *eusebeia*, and *theosebeia* in the New Testament, reached the conclusion that the whole concept of "religion" (obviously, as understood in that particular theological tradition) is alien to the Bible and that in the mother tongue of the New Testament authors there was no linguistic equivalent for these Greek terms.[14] This last remark, as already observed, is true of *all* oriental religions, and should have thrown doubt on the very concept of religion employed here!

It is, therefore, hardly surprising that many good dictionaries of biblical theology (e.g., that of Dufour or Bauer) would have no column on "religion." From "redemption" they pass on to "remnant"—indeed a symbolic *saltus*, suggesting another possible concept of religion that could be extracted from the Bible! Regrettably, it is under the aforesaid category of "religion" that all non-Christian soteriologies are subsumed and dismissed in favor of biblical faith.

In the militant stream of liberation theology, this Barthian view of religion dovetails neatly with Marx's equally evangelistic and Eurocentric evaluation of religions and cultures. Though many a Latin American critic has succeeded in pushing the Marxian analysis to the opposite conclusion—namely, that religion could be a "leaven of liberation rather than an opiate"—an Asian sensitivity is still necessary to monitor the Occidentalist bias of this new Marxist view.[15]

Marx, whose contribution to the liberation of Third World nations dare never be underestimated, does not, for that reason, cease to be a man of his own time and clime: a nineteenth-century European. A writer who revels in revealing the racial and class prejudices of Marx and Engels concludes:

> Their attitudes were typical attitudes of the nineteenth-century Europeans who, regardless of their ideology, thought in terms of a hierarchy of cultures with their own at the top and who occasionally used biology to provide a scientific basis for their categorization of societies into higher and lower forms.[16]

The late Lelio Basso, the Italian Marxist theoretician, acknowledged this deficiency with laudable frankness.[17] Let me cite a few of his well-documented observations.

In Marx's *Manifesto*, the whole idea of "progress" and "civilization" is simply equated with the Westernization of the East, the urbanization of the countryside, and the proletarianization of the peasantry—all in the name of socialism! And in *Capital*, the European form of capitalist industrialization is envisaged as the model for the rest of the world, an indispensable prelude to the proletarian revolution. For this reason, Engels rejoiced at the American aggression in Mexico and the subsequent annexation of rich provinces such as California. He also applauded the French acquisition of Algeria—though he did have second thoughts about it. Similarly, Marx welcomed the British conquest of India because the breakdown of the ancient Indian civilization, followed preferably by europeanization, seemed an indispensable condition for the building up of a modern industrial culture. That there could, in fact, be a non-Western, non-European way to socialism culturally based on the peasant communes of the *obscina* was of course proposed and debated at length even before the October Revolution; but in this regard, Marx, and especially Engels, did not really shed their Western chauvinism.

Lenin's postrevolutionary policies seem to have further entrenched this occidentalism in the orthodox stream of classic Marxism. After gaining power he not only tried to expedite the industrialization of the U.S.S.R. (supposedly on a state basis rather than on a capitalist basis) but tried also to bring about socialism *from the top*, vertically, with little faith in the process of allowing it to emerge from the people, from below. In "accelerating the historical process," as it is called, many extraneous elements had to be imposed on the people, with a good deal of violence to their religious and cultural sensitivities. One should not forget that Lenin (perhaps influenced by Černyševskij's ideal of destroying the Asian character of the Russian people—the *Aziatična* as it was called) introduced a steam-roller socialism that ruthlessly sought to level down the religious and cultural identities of a people. The cry for proletarian *internationalism*—valid in itself—was in practice a zeal for *occidentalism*. In this he excelled the Western missionaries of his time who preached a "universal gospel," which in reality was their own narrow European version of it! The Brezhnev principle is a variation of this intransigent verticalism.

It is true that Lenin made many theoretical concessions to other ways of socialism as verified, for instance, in the case of Mongolia, as modern Marxist apologists observe with pride.[18] But denying to the founders of Marxism the right to be men of their own times does not help. Would that a massive effort be made to purge Marxism of its eurocentrism and cultural colonialism! It should revise its notion of Afro-Asian religions and cultures in terms of their liberative potentialities and discover indigenous ways to socialism—the kind of aggiornamento inaugurated by Markov, Ernst, and other Marxist intellectuals of the Leipzig school—vis-à-vis the precapitalist societies of Africa.[19] Such a corrective measure, moreover, has already been anticipated in the political praxis of Africans themselves. Amilcar Cabral's Marxism is a case in point.[20] One could also cite with some reservation Lumumba and Nkrumah. Asia has Ho Chi Minh. They wrote little and transmitted much to posterity through their praxis, which therefore serves as a *locus theologicus* for those groping for a liberation theology of religions and cultures.

This Afro-Asian critique of Marxist occidentalism is also an implicit judgment on the militant stream of Latin American theology, which maintains a methodological continuity with Western Marxism and a cultural continuity with European theology. Their Latin and Marxist idiom does not permit the ethnic identity of racial minorities to be reflected in their theology. Amerindians, blacks, and Asiatics—almost a fifth of the Latin American population—are absolute majorities in certain provinces.[21] Has their unique community sense (e.g., the Indian *cofradías*, which are alleged to be a rich cultural alternative to Latin *hermandades*)[22] made a visible impact on the ecclesiological revolution of basic communities?[23]

I agree with the Marxists who hold that a conflict between ethnic struggles and class struggles could jeopardize the total liberation of a people. But this fear—if it is coupled with the Marxist tendency to confuse internationalism with occidentalism—could be an excuse for reinforcing Latinism. As a matter of fact, racism remains a contemporary problem, not a mere thing of the colonial past.[24] Not surprisingly, even the Marxist Lipschütz, who conceded that these non-Latin ethnic groups could form self-governing "linguistic" republics, would not think of a hypothetically socialist nation of Latin America except in Hispano-American terms, always having the Soviet model before him,[25] a model not entirely free of Russian cultural and linguistic colonialism.[26] It is, therefore, heartening to note that participants in the São Paulo conference did touch on this delicate question, though in the Final Document they skirted the subject, giving it only a passing nod.[27]

Liberation and Inculturation: History of a Tension

Some theologians display an exaggerated solicitude for inculturation, because of which they stand open to severe judgment, especially when the historical context of the liberation/inculturation tension is brought into focus. Diagram 2 does precisely this by tabulating the three successive versions of the two christological perspectives: the Christ-*against*-religions theology and Christ-*of*-religions theology. The table is self-explanatory, and I shall here only skim over the three phases, touching down only on salient points.

Phase 1 covers the era of Euro-ecclesiastical expansionism, when the colonialist Christ was set on a warring spree against false religions in the lands now called the Third World. Not even De Nobili and Ricci contested this Christ-*against*-religions theology! They only questioned the policy of imposing Western civilization as a means of conversion, a policy that prevailed despite their protest, and persists to this day in subtle ways (phases 2 and 3). The theological breakthrough began perhaps in the nineteenth century with the epiphany of the gnostic Christ, who appeared in the works of both Hindu and Christian theologians.[28]

Some of these Christian theologians anticipated the later official doctrine of the Lambeth Conference (1930) and the Second Vatican Council—namely, that Christ works in other religions as the final consummation of all human aspiration for redemption. Obviously this "fulfillment theory of religions," even in its post-Vatican II versions, is fraught with intrinsic theological difficulties that need not be discussed here. Suffice it to note that it is an abstract theory that excludes from religious disclosure the basic theme of any genuine theology: the poor. After all, is not the story of Jesus preeminently the story of a God *of* the poor, a God *with* the poor, a God *for* the poor? No wonder that in the 1960s, with the sharpening of Third World consciousness, the nexus between the religions and the poor began to receive articulate attention.

Thus begins phase 2, with its own version of the two theological perspectives. Enter first the neocolonialist Christ in the person of the missionary with a jeep. Western "civilization" now yields place to Western "development" as the medium of Christ's saving presence. I even remember its being called pre-evangelization! How could other religions relieve the poor in their plight if those religions themselves are the partial cause of a people's underdevelopment, and if technology and progress are unique Christian achievements destined to free the non-Christian masses from their superstitious traditions?[29] That the non-Christian worldview could provide a saner philosophy of development,[30] as illustrated, for instance, by the Sarvodaya movement in its earlier phase, or that, in the process of "modernization," the evangelical values of other religions and cultures were being immolated on the altar of mammon, were still the opinions of a dissenting minority.[31]

A counterthesis to developmentalism, however, did come from the Christ-*of*-religions theology. It found an anchor in the numerous ashrams and their equivalents already in existence for decades. They embodied the spirit of renunciation central to many cultures, thus expressing their solidarity with both the poor and their religions. Material progress need not necessarily mean human development, nor is material poverty in itself human impoverishment. The ashramic Christ fought neither of these. His sole attack was on that which caused such polarity: greed, the demon *within*, an enemy of all authentic spirituality.

And there was the rub. The *organized* character of greed passed unnoticed. While the war was waged and even won *within* the walls of ashrams, the poor—the waste product of the earth's capital-accumulating plutocracy—continued to grow in number and misery. Could their struggle for sheer survival succeed if that sinful system was not a target of their struggle? Unless stained by the stigma of solidarity with that struggle, monastic poverty will always remain a shallow status symbol of a client-gathering guru. The claim to have renounced wealth is vanity of vanities if those who have no wealth to renounce cannot benefit from it. There is a precedent in Jesus, in his precursor John, and in Gandhi, his Hindu admirer, for whom voluntary poverty was not only a renunciation of mammon in the micro-ethical sphere of one's soul, but a denunciation of its stooges in the macro-ethical order of politico-religious institutions.

It is sad that whereas yesterday's feudalism turned some monasteries into oases of plenty amid deserts of poverty, pushing them into the hands of today's revolutionaries who *force* monks to practice *voluntary* poverty for the benefit of the masses (as has happened in Tibet and Mongolia), today's capitalism has entrenched some ashrams, zendos, and prayer centers in the grip of wealth-accumulating patrons who frequent them for spells of tranquility and return unconverted and unrepentant, awaiting another revolution to disrupt that unholy alliance with mammon. Have we not also heard of mystics spinning dollars by exporting meditation to the West? Like rubber, coffee, and copper, our spirituality too gets processed in the West and returns with expensive price tags and sophisticated labels ("Transcendental Meditation") to be consumed locally! Who is the beneficiary? And what of the horror of caste and sexist discrimination that thrives on religious sanction? How many prayer centers have cared or dared to go against the grain? The ashramic Christ seemed no more sensitive to the demands of justice than did the neocolonialist Christ.

It is, therefore, worth noting that phase 3 dawned during a period when the pendulum of politics poised for a brief passing moment on the left extremity before it began its present rightward swing with the massive crisis in the socialist states and the rise of Reaganism. Disappointment with doctrinaire theologies and disillusionment with both the developmentalism and "mysticism" of the previous era added fuel to the fire of mounting liberation fever in the expanding circles of Christian activists in our part of the world. It was at this time that Latin American theology (equated here with liberation theology), with ten years of maturity behind it, began to awaken the Afro-Asian "indigenizers" from their ethnocentric stupor, just as it had earlier shocked the Euro-American theoreticians from their dogmatic slumber. It is understandable that some Asian theologians with leftist leanings began to sing the liberation song out of beat with the non-Latin rhythm of their own cultures. The "lord of the dance" was the liberator Christ who redeemed the poor not only from their poverty but also from their traditional religions, which sustained the sinful systems. It is therefore equally understandable that the incarnate Christ of the inculturationists stood aghast on the opposite pole!

Just as one particular stream of liberation theology pursues, even today, the colonial evangelism of the past—as was shown in "The Liberation Thesis" above—so also the bulk of literature churned out in ever proliferating seminars on inculturation does not show any significant departure from the previous era's narrow focus on religion and culture. It pays scant attention to the colossal scandal of institutionalized misery that poses a challenge to every religion.

A defensive posture adopted against the liberationist thesis may partly explain such blindness. The implications of this limitation are serious and I have spelled them out clearly elsewhere.[32] Nevertheless, I shall resume this discussion in the second half of this chapter, after dealing with the liberative and revolutionary potentials of non-Christian religions—something that both liberationists (the school I am criticizing here) and inculturationists have failed to discern, but which is the very texture of a Third World theology of religions.

TOWARD A THIRD WORLD THEOLOGY OF RELIGIONS

Anatomy of Religion in the Third World

Every theologian should be alerted to the fact that a substantial amount of information regarding religions and cultures in the Third World is gathered, processed, and distributed by Euro-American research centers. The First World still has a monopoly on the resources required for such studies—money and media, academic prestige and personnel. Even the highly acclaimed "participatory observation method" in anthropology has been unmasked as another arm of Western dominance.[33]

The occidentalist bias that liberation theology has absorbed from a tradition traceable to Marx and Barth is only the tip of the iceberg. There are deeper predispositions acquired by all of us—myself included—in the course of our intellectual training: we are all dependent on these same sources for our understanding of the religious phenomenon in its global magnitude.

As Evans-Pritchard noted, generations of writers on religion (Taylor, Frazer, Malinowski, Durkheim, Freud, and their followers), in their sincere search for truth, were only reacting against the religion of their upbringing.[34] In the face of their attempts to explain religion by explaining it away, theologians such as Barth tried to save Christianity by lifting it above the realm of religion, indirectly offering a biblico-theological prop to such antireligion theories.

C. E. Stipe has diagnosed the malaise of Western anthropologists as "functionalism," which tends to gloss over religion as something redundant in the cultures they study.[35] Taking the focal aspect of religion to be something outside natural, human experience, they perceive the rite, not the system of meaning and beliefs. They study social relationships without due regard to the worldview that religions provide.

An interesting case is that of Sierksma accusing Lanternari of leaving anthropology in favor of theology[36] because the latter merely observed Christianity to be transcendent, unlike the messianic movements, more interested in human salvation on earth.[37] Marxian interpretation of Mau Mau as purely Kenyan nationalism or Melanesian cargo cults as purely economic phenomena shares in this Western reductionism. According to Stipe, this is precisely what hinders Western anthropologists from assessing the role of religion in relation to cultural change.[38]

Is not the same bias keeping the theologian (liberationist or inculturationist) from perceiving religion in positive terms of liberation struggles and revolutionary change? I recommend that a critical discernment be exercised in pursuing available studies on religions and that fieldwork on this subject be undertaken afresh from within the Third World perspective of peoples struggling for integral human liberation. It is with this forewarning that I wish to describe the anatomy of the religious phenomenon in the Third World.

The intricate network of religions and cultures that spreads across the Third World baffles the theologian as much as it does the anthropologist. To do more than trace its major contours would, therefore, be unpragmatic within the limitations of this chapter. Nor should I spend time on definitions of religion and culture—an academic pastime that has bred confusion in the West. We who breathe religion as our normal atmosphere would rather go by the first intuitive and experiential grasp of what it means in life. Therefore, without formulating definitions for ourselves, we can still detect the ones that are wrong!

The first observation is that religion and culture coincide fully in tribal societies practically everywhere in the Third World. Culture is the variegated expression of religion. But because religions meet each other always in and through their respective cultural self-manifestations, there result subtle differentiations between religions and cultures. Thus, one might speak about several cultures within one religion and, conversely, about several religions within one culture. The former case is exemplified in the three missionary religions: Buddhism, Islam, and Christianity (listed here in descending order of cultural differentiation). As for cultures that accommodate several religions, a whole series can be cited—for example, Buddhism and Hinduism in Nepal, Taoism and Confucianism in China, Buddhism and Shintoism in Japan, Hinduism and Islam in Java.

In some instances, the culture of one religion relates to the other as host to guest. Hence these terms possess the conceptual elasticity that the complexity of reality has bequeathed on them. For reasons that are implicit in my prefatory remarks above, I am here primarily speaking about religions as the pivotal point of reference, and obliquely about culture. This premised, let me attempt to sort out the various strands of religiousness that have been woven into the exquisite cultural fabric of the Third World. Actually one can discern at least three of them; the crisscrossing of racio-linguistic contours within the so-called scriptural religions must be mentioned first.

/.   The so-called scriptural or book religions of the world have all taken their origin from three reservoirs of Asian spirituality, each having its own racio-linguistic idiom: the Semitic (Judaism, Islam, and Christianity), the Indian (Hinduism, Jainism, and Buddhism), and the Chinese (Taoism and Confucianism). These streams of religiousness have not confined themselves to the neighborhood of their sources, but have been meandering beyond their linguistic boundaries, even across continents, thus flooding the world—Asia in particular—with a plethora of hybrid cultures.

For instance, Islam's Semitic religiousness pervades both the Malayo-Polynesian and the Indo-Aryan cultures of Indonesia and Pakistan, respectively, and also permeates many African tribes. Hinduism has a firm grip on the lives of both Dravidian and Indo-Aryan peoples of India, besides serving as the subterranean foundation for many Southeast Asian civilizations. Buddhism, which preserves its original Indian format only in Sri Lanka, has shaped several cultures by allowing itself to be shaped by them, with the result that one hears of Ural-Altaic, Malayo-Polynesian, Sino-Tibetan, Japanese, and Indo-Aryan versions of Buddhist culture. Christianity too can make a few modest claims in this regard.

ﾕ.   The second type of cross-fertilization takes place between these religions and tribal religions. As a matter of fact it coincides with the process by which, as described above, a scriptural religion acquires citizenship in another linguistic zone. Regrettably, our theological manuals that deal with non-Christian religions focus mostly on these scriptural religions, or what sociologists call "the great traditions." But the peasantry and the proletariat of the Third World are, for the most part, bearers of a nonscriptural or regionalized traditional religiousness either *within* the framework of a major religion (so-called popular Buddhism, popular Taoism, popular Hinduism, and, as in Latin America, popular religion) or *totally outside* any scriptural religion (e.g., tribal religions not yet proselytized by the former). This is why I urged at the Asian Theological Consultation in Sri Lanka, 1979, that due attention be paid to these religions.[39] Their beliefs and practices have not frozen into written formulas but flow with time, thus exhibiting the *flexibility essential for social change*. This is the first corollary I wish to underline here, for future reference.

Inasmuch as all scriptural religions began as oral traditions, and traditional religions of today are bound, sooner or later, to express their sacred heritage also in written form, I prefer to use two other terms that I have already employed in other chapters of this volume: metacosmic (not to be confused with acosmic) and cosmic.[40] The former type of religion defines its soteriology in terms of a metacosmic "beyond" capable of being internalized as the salvific "within" of the human person, either through the agapeic path of redeeming love or through the gnostic way of liberative knowledge—this being the major difference between the biblical religions and most nonbiblical ones. Cosmic religions, as the term indicates, revolve around cosmic powers—normally rendered as "gods," "deities," "spirits" in English. They refer to natural phenomena (often personified) as well as the spirits of past heroes and one's own ancestors, not excluding "departed souls" and "saints" in popular Christianity. For this reason Confucianism is to be classed as a cosmic religion despite its scriptural base.

Further, wherever the two species of religiousness have merged, the common people's genius has created a synthesis that a superficial observer might mistake for syncretism. That is why Richard Gombrich has suggested the word "accretism" to describe such mergers, for in the hybrid cultures that issue from this symbiosis, *homo religiosus* learns to align locally determined cosmic concerns (food, harvest, rain and sunshine, floods and drought, health and sickness, life and death, marriage and politics) with the soteriological orientation of his or her life toward a metacosmic Beyond.[41] One welcomes, therefore, the bidisciplinary approach of scripture scholars (Dumont, Bechert, Gombrich, among others) who turn to anthropology in order to respect the hermeneutical reciprocity between book and beliefs, scripture and tradition, written text and living context. Popular hermeneusis of ancient lore reveals the peoples' ongoing creative response to contemporary reality. This is the second corollary I wish to put on record.

This phenomenon of accretism points also to a third corollary. No major *3.* religion could have traveled beyond its seat of origin and become incarnate in the lives of the masses had it not sent its roots deep into the popular religiousness of each tribe and race.[42] In other words, historically and phenomenologically speaking, there cannot be a metacosmic religiousness having an institutional grip on the people save on the basis of a popular religiousness! The converse, however, is not true. For there can be and in fact there are tribal religions independent of, though open to, scriptural religions.

The patterns of mass conversion offer us a fourth and important corollary. *4.* As stated elsewhere, mass conversions from one soteriology to another are rare, if not impossible, except under military pressure.[43] But a changeover from a tribal religion to a metacosmic soteriology is a spontaneous process in which the former, without sacrificing its own character, provides a popular base for the latter. Being cosmic religions, they are this-worldly in every sense of the term and are often drawn by some "community advantages" to accept the institutional framework of a scriptural religion.[44] (The latter, which generally shuns change, tends paradoxically to use its other-worldly teachings to consolidate its this-worldly institutions!)

The scheduled castes and tribes in India that have accepted Christianity, or more particularly Buddhism and Islam, on a massive scale substantiate this thesis. A better illustration is provided by the missionary conflicts between Christianity and Islam. After three and a half centuries of concerted proselytism, colonial Christianity in Indonesia collected only a little over two million converts from Islam, most of whom came from northern Sumatra, Moluccas, Ambonia, and other outer islands where tribal culture prevailed. Christian "successes" among tribal peoples of the Atlantic coast of Africa—compared with the miserable failure in Muslim Africa, except for a minor conquest among mountain tribes in Kabyles[45]—point in the same direction.

Let me end with a fifth and final corollary. Tribal and clan societies, given their strong religio-cultural cohesion, are never immune to the danger of intertribal conflicts. Tribalism—often equated with divisive provincialism—can be exploited ideologically by the enemies of social change. The strategy of "divide and rule" can thwart liberation movements, as will be discussed in the next section.

To sum up, I have described the anatomy of the religious phenomenon first in terms of the crisscrossing of racio-linguistic contours within scriptural religions, and, secondly, in terms of the five consequences issuing from the accretion of cosmic into metacosmic religions.

There is another interaction that deserves attention if the picture is to be complete: the interaction between these religions and various socio-political ideologies. This brings me to the core of my inquiry: religion and revolution.

The Revolutionary Urge in Religions and the Role of Ideologies

Lunacharsky, the first Soviet minister of culture, had this confession to make about religion: "It is like a nail," he declared, "the harder you hit it, the deeper it goes into the wood."[46] By persecuting religion, revolutionaries hardly kill it but only make it more reactionary. Conversely, when challenged by an oppressive system, religion finds occasion to unleash its potential for radical change.

A true revolution cannot go against religion in its totality. If a revolution succeeds, it does so normally as a cathartic renewal of religion itself. Such a statement is based on the experience of seven decades of Marxism. Che Guevara sensed the same thing when he said: "Only when Christians have the courage to give a wholehearted revolutionary testimony will the Latin American revolution become invincible."[47] With this prophecy he seems to have suggested the theme for a new chapter in the history of both Marxist ideology and the Christian religion—a chapter that Nicaragua is presently struggling at death point to write for posterity!

This is even more true of the other religions that have a more extensive hold on the Third World than does Christianity. No *true* liberation is possible unless persons are "religiously motivated" toward it. To be religiously motivated is to be drawn from the depths of one's being. This motivation, I concede, could be occasioned by alien ideologies, as history has often attested. But the peoples of the Third World will not spontaneously embark on a costly adventure unless their lives are touched and their depths stirred by its prospects *along the "cultural" patterns of their own "religious" histories*—which, of course, differ widely from place to place, as was demonstrated in the previous section.

Take, for instance, the Chinese peasant culture, marked by a history of revolts, in contrast with the culture of the Guinean peasantry, which has had no such tradition—a fact explicitly noted by Amilcar Cabral, who laid great emphasis on the local cultural variants of every socialist revolution.[48] This did not imply for Cabral that Guinea was incapable of radical change but that he had to consult his own culture rather than merely copy an alien model. Let us therefore first look at the African situation, for it offers many lessons to Third World theologians.

Islam and Christianity in Africa

If Marx is rightly interpreted, the tribal communities of Africa can be classed as "precapitalist socialist societies" in that they can reach full-fledged socialism without passing through the crucible of capitalism.[49] Jean Ziegler, with World Bank statistics, tries to vindicate the Tanzanian experiment of Julius Nyerere in favor of this theory.[50] But this is no easy task; both colonial and indigenous elements have left *ideological* dents in these societies. I refer to the local bourgeoisie and the feudal barons (not to mention the white settlers in Rhodesia and South Africa!) who inherited power from colonial rulers so that even progressive patriots such as Lumumba and Nkrumah could not radically change the basic character of the *nationalist* liberation movements.

Mozambique gives us the other alternative—if I may agree with Sergio Vieira, himself a member of FRELIMO (National Liberation Front of Mozambique) and a government minister.[51] Portugal, unlike Britain, Belgium, and France, had good reasons not to give even "flag independence" to its colonies but to cling to a fascist rule, thus inviting armed struggle.[52] Mozambique and Angola responded. The arbitrary demarcation of the future frontiers of African "nations" by the colonialists, which increased racial and tribal fragmentation, and the local exploitation of tribal loyalties (corollary 5, above) were attacked simultaneously in order to bring patriotism in line with intertribal proletarianism, as shown in the Mozambique people's massive self-immolation for the liberation of Zimbabwe.[53] This is an African response to one ideology in repudiation of another. This process as illustrated in Mozambique is bound to be generally normative in the future, because Africa is, by far, the most exploited of continents.

This is the background against which the role of scriptural religions should be assessed. Of course in Africa there are only two candidates for the conversion contest: Islam and Christianity. Because the rule of the game is "first come, first served," a tribal society that has already given its allegiance to one will not normally withdraw it in favor of the other (corollary 4). Hence, with most of tribal Africa divided between Islam and Christianity, we can expect one of three things, if not all of them: a disastrous confrontation, a defensive compromise, or a daring collaboration between the two religions. The first is *not* unlikely; the last is imperative—provided one knows wherein collaboration is desired. Let me comment on each alternative.

Why confrontation? The Christianity of the colonial masters, which still dominates the African church, is institutionally handicapped because of its history of hostilities with Islam in Europe and in the missions.[54] It is humbled before Islam's credibility in the movement for African unity. It is hampered by its reluctance to disengage its ecclesiastical loyalties from the ideological grip of the countries of its provenance. And it is pastorally inhibited by its dread of liberation struggles. Hence, unless thoroughly revolutionized—that is to say, substituted by an indigenous alternative—it is bound to become overdefensive in the face of Islam. God forbid that it should summon all available external help to consolidate itself against its rival. Have not Rhodesia and South Africa given a precedent? The other alternative might be compromise through "dialogue"—the dubious type of dialogue that is insidiously fostered and even financed by various ideological blocs, a dangerous compromise that blunts the liberative edge of both religions.

Common sense dictates, therefore, that the climate be created for harnessing the religious zeal of both traditions into a prophetic movement in the service of God's poor, through a socio-political collaboration in a common *theopraxis of liberation*. This obviously presupposes an unbiased Christian acquaintance with Islam.

Islam in Iran

Let Christians step back and gauge Islam's gigantic stature as it stands with self-confidence at the portals of the Third World, where it remains the most widespread single religious force to reckon with. Christians are made to believe by the media that it is also a generator of religious fanaticism and fundamentalism. Khomeini is the obvious symbol that springs to their mind. Why not focus, then, precisely on Iran and see where the fanatics come from and how a revolution is born?

Scan the last hundred years of history, pleads Eqbal Ahmed, Pakistani scholar, and you will note that the Khomeini episode is the *eighth* major battle that the Muslim nation has embarked on to defend its sovereignty against mercantile and military exploiters from the West![55] Religious clerics were in the thick of the struggle. Reuter's concession (1872) and the tobacco concession to Major Talbot (1895) were the first two Western maneuvers. The third uprising was in 1905 against D'Arcy's concession to open Iran's oil resources to the West—as before, with the monarch's collaboration. This revolt succeeded in bringing about a modern constitutional government in 1906, which was soon overthrown by Czarist Russia and Britain in 1911. The opposition gathered momentum by 1919 against Lord Curzon's Anglo-Persian Treaty that would have turned Iran into a British colony, in fact if not in name. This fourth national victory lasted only two years. The British maneuvered a coup d'etat led by Reza Khan in 1921. Thus absolute monarchy was reestablished with Khan as dictator, the father of the notorious ex-shah.

Reza Khan was praised in the Western press for ushering in "modernization and westernization under the aegis of foreign domination," adds Ahmed. The Nationalists did throw him out in 1941 but could not regain control of the administration, for the British maintained a regency while the future shah grew up under colonial tutelage. The Nationalists staged a return in 1950 and, after a struggle, forced new elections (under the 1906 Constitution) and established the Mossadegh government, which eventually nationalized the oil resources of Iran.

Then came Iran's nightmare: the CIA organized a coup d'etat against the Mossadegh government in 1953 and installed the shah, the tyrant who massacred nearly two hundred thousand Iranians—among them poets and writers. "Iran's wealth was looted, transferred, and spent in the West." Iran's Muslim masses did not simply fight the shah. They fought the superpower that forced him to be its gendarme in the Persian Gulf, sold him $19 billion worth of weapons, and supported his repressions until the last murderous days of his reign.

Who were the fanatics? Who were the liberators? Is this also the future of the ASEAN countries with a restless Muslim majority, and of Pakistan, which are all in the hands of the same powers that provoked the wrath of Iran? And what of the Soviet intervention in Afghanistan—understandable in the light of capitalist aggression, but no less abominable? Islam *is* a giant, and *not* a sleeping one.

Hinduism in India

My third example is Hinduism—a great religion comprising many little religions, inscrutable even to the expert who can concentrate only on one little corner of the maze. With the revolutionary urge of religions as my particular focus, I can still make valid observations illustrative of principles enunciated above (especially corollaries 1, 2, and 3).

First, Hinduism can be taken as a metacosmic soteriology centered around the sacred texts of revealed and interpreted truths (*Śruti* and *Smṛti*). It is from within this orthodox tradition that the Indian renaissance took off as a reform movement, stimulated by the challenge of Western Christianity. Despite its social influences and theological adventures (including the discovery of the gnostic Christ alluded to above), it did not cease to be elitist.

According to one sociological survey, the offshoots of this movement have now withered into devotionalist sects. Some sects of the north and west of India have succumbed to political rightism and xenophobic chauvinism. Even god-men cults seem an apolitical middle-class phenomenon, indeed a far cry from the medieval savior cults, which were "liberational." Perhaps in reaction to the onslaught of urbanization, these new cults show a marked shift from the classic concern with liberation to a mere quest for meaningfulness as in affluent societies elsewhere.[56] Besides, the most disturbing issue of caste discrimination—a socio-economic slavery "religiously" enforced by Brahmanic orthodoxy—is not squarely faced in these reforms.

To watch the transition from reform to revolution, one must, therefore, move away from this orthodox center of Brahmanic Hinduism. The bhakti movement, the *Dalit Sāhitya* ("Writings of the oppressed"), and the tribal revolts represent three grades in this centrifugal trend.

The bhakti movement—initially a popular tendency on the fringes of

Brahmanism—"is the most creative upsurge of the Indian mind," which has inspired "several social and political revolts . . . from Shivaji's rebellion in the seventeenth century to Mahatma Gandhi's in the twentieth."[57] A comparative study of two such movements in Maharashtra helps bring out the ingredients of a *religious* revolt against caste and sexist discrimination.[58] The first is the Mahanubhava movement inaugurated by Chakradhar (1194–1276) who, in his ruthless denunciation of Brahman orthodoxy, did not spare even the Vedic scriptures. The fellowship it fostered offered equality of status to both the 'sudras and women. Chakradhar, of course, was killed for it. Yet the movement (revived only recently) could not muster popular enthusiasm, because it was conservatively monastic and relatively removed from grassroot struggles. Its message too suffered in that the mode of transmission was limited to the written word, a medium totally inaccessible to the illiterate masses.

Contrast this with the Warkari movement, which spread wider, grew deeper, and survived persecution by going underground. It was a lay initiative with a popular base and truly a movement of the oppressed: the untouchable castes. It produced a galaxy of revolutionary poet-saints, many of whom were martyred—counterparts of the Hebrew prophets. In India's religious ethos, a reformer, in order to arouse the masses, must also be a poet and a saint. The other secret of success, clearly exemplified in the Warkari movement, is the use of the oral medium for transmitting the message. Such a medium necessarily brings about a personal encounter between the mutually inspiring agents of social change: the suffering masses and the poet-saint. A vast production of oral literature and the extensive use of dance and song ensured an ongoing program of "conscientization." It never petrified into a written text but ever remained fluid and flowing with the passage of time. Even the sacred lore of the ancients, whenever cited or insinuated in their freedom songs, went through a creative popular hermeneusis. In their later encounters with Islam and Christianity they also displayed a spirit of humane ecumenicity.

Circulating for two decades now, the *Dalit Sāhitya* ("Writings of the oppressed"), on the other hand, constitute an ideological departure from the bhakti movement of which it still is a historical continuation.[59] A greater openness to other revolutionary ideologies has given teeth to this movement of popular writers, which at first had been a mere conscientization exercise within popular religion. Marx, Lenin, Mao, Che, Ho Chi Minh, and Martin Luther King, Jr., figure prominently in these writings, for the Dalits feel themselves associated with the liberation struggles of all the world's oppressed. From openness to all that is liberative in other religions, there has grown a new openness to other secular ideologies. Thus the bhakti movement has lent itself to be used ideologically to destroy the oppressive religious system in which it still has its roots![60]

As we come to tribal India, we have not merely moved to the fringe of Brahmanic religiousness, but to *another* religious system *outside* it. The student of Indology is not often introduced to this reality. It is, no doubt, a precapitalist socialism that we meet again, in contrast with the feudalism of monastic religions (e.g., Buddhism) and of theocratic religions (e.g., Brahmanism). Yet, as in Africa, so even more in India, feudalistic tendencies are gradually seeping into tribal societies.[61] It is said that although the tribal and the untouchable caste woman often enjoys equality with the male because of her relative economic independence, the adoption of Hindu values are tending to diminish the status of the harijan woman.[62]

Wherever it is found, tribal society is egalitarian, free of caste and class, for it is based on a *religious socialism* that is uninhibited by puritanical mores characteristic of scriptural religions but prone to counterviolence if defense of the community requires it. No wonder, as Gail Omvedt documents, that the tribals as a whole can boast of a history of nationalist and class struggles all over Asia including India, not to speak of the bandit tradition of "Robin Hoods" who rob wealthy landowners with the poor Indian villagers applauding as spectators.[63]

Buddhism in China

Let me conclude this survey with an extensive note on Buddhism, for it is a pan-Asian religion occupying a position analogous to that of Islam in the Third World.

It is common knowledge that the Buddhist scriptures demand radical social change but lend no support to violent struggles, even though naive theories about "righteous killing" have been advanced in the course of Buddhist history.[64] But tradition makes up for scripture, and it does so extravagantly! Here even orthodox Buddhism has to its credit a theory and praxis of rebellion. Some scholars warn that it is only when Buddhism as a religion is challenged in the midst of political chaos that monks come to the forefront with lay support, as in Thailand.[65]

But what about Burma's Buddhist resurgence, which was messianically political? Initially aimed at Burmese kings, it was later directed toward their British successors. There must have been about twenty revolts from 1838 to 1928—all inspired by the Maitreya cult: the eschatological expectation of a just social order to be ushered in with the appearance of the future Buddha. It is a belief that has scriptural foundation. Note also that it was this wave of Buddhist rebellions that brought to the surface the later independence movement with which U Nu, a philo-Marxist initially, tried his abortive experiment with "Buddhist socialism."[66] Sri Lanka and Indochina have followed similar patterns. Vietnam's history of the Li dynasty and the concept of emperor-monk reflect a militantly political Buddhism that is no less virulent today.

Not surprisingly, revolutionary praxis on the fringes of the Buddhist institution shows greater radicalism. China offers us a series of persuasive examples, of which I make here a random selection.[67] From about A.D. 402 there were about ten armed rebellions organized by monks, climaxing in A.D. 515 with that of Fa-K'ing, a revolutionary monk who, like many of his kind, married a nun. These monastic rebellions were directed against both the state and the official religious establishment. Since then there have been many messianic sects that had a popular base, clearly indicating the influence of cosmic religion over metacosmic. One such was the Maitreya sect founded in A.D. 610 by a Buddhist monk who declared himself emperor. This sect had incorporated into its belief system the cult of Buddha Amitābha and the desire for rebirth in his heaven known as the Western Paradise. The adherents of this sect maintained that this paradise should be created on earth, here and now, rather than in a remote future. They wished to bring about a Buddha-land, a state of peace and equity in this existence. This sect left its traces in the whole period from the seventh to the sixteenth centuries.

The White Cloud sect (between 1108 and 1300) and the Lo sect (1505–1956) were two others of the same kind. The most significant, perhaps, is the White Lotus sect (*Pai-Lien Ts'ai*, 1133–1813), a branch of which continued under the name *I-Kuam-Tao* as late as 1956 and was hunted down by the Maoist regime. The founder was a Buddhist monk named Mao tzu-Yuan (1086–1166), who was assisted by women and married monks—something that provoked the wrath of the orthodox sangha. But these movements continued to enjoy a certain amount of popular support. Mao tzu-Yuan was exiled and the movement proscribed several times; then it was once more recognized by Emperor Jen T'sing (1312–1321). Among its many revolutions, the most successful was that of 1351 under the leadership of Han Shan-T'ung, who also called himself Buddha Maitreya. This revolution succeeded in destroying the Mongol rule and established a new dynasty—the Ming dynasty. Its first emperor was Chu-Yuang-Chang, ex-Buddhist novice and a former officer of the White Lotus army. The irony was that he later turned anti-Buddhist. This movement was crushed again in 1813. The ban was removed in 1911, and a branch of it, as indicated above, was active as late as 1956.

By Marxist standards these were not real revolutions; they could at best be classed as rebellions. But they show how Buddhists could respond to the revolutionary moods and creeds of the time. In these instances, the Buddhist messianic interpretation of the scriptures and the scriptural justification of "revolution" had come as a response to a contemporary ideology springing from the Taoist secret societies that awaited the true ruler who was to give great peace to those awaiting him, and from the Confucianist expectation of the enlightened emperor.

What I wish to underscore here is that Buddhists living in a particular historical situation may, under the influence of non-Buddhist ideologies and movements, reinterpret their scriptural sources in order to respond creatively to a contemporary need—even if it means a costly revolution. This tradition continues to this day in Chinese Buddhism.

Religion and Revolution in a Third World Theology

In scanning the wide expanse of non-Christian cultures in the Third World, I have cast a searchlight on only four areas: African religiousness (which resembles that of Oceania), west Asian Islam, south Asian Hinduism, and east Asian Buddhism. Though by no means exhaustive, these four samples are illustrative of some of the major features of religiousness in the Third World and support three overall conclusions.

1. Outside the pale of Semitic monotheism, there is perhaps only one stream of religiousness (one form of Hinduism) that regards the one ultimate reality as a personal being who summons the cosmos into existence and summons human beings to a personal, redeeming encounter with the divine self. A God who is one, personal, absolute creator-redeemer of the world and of humankind is neither universally affirmed nor universally denied. Religiousness—especially in Asia—is for a greater part of humanity metatheistic, or at least nontheistic, if not, at times, explicitly atheistic. The common thrust, however, remains *soteriological*, the concern of most religions being *liberation* (*vimukti, moksa,* nirvana) rather than speculation about a hypothetical liberator. Many metacosmic religions point to a future that is attainable as the present moment of total human emancipation, putting the accent on a metapersonal Beyond, if not on an "impersonal" but transphenomenal It: Tao, dharma, *tathatā, Brahman,* nirvana. The cosmic religions, on the other hand, look up to many gods and spiritual forces, which constitute the spectrum of a complex unity of being enveloping the whole of human cosmic existence. Even where the two forms of religion—the cosmic and metacosmic—merge, the net result is not a simple equivalent of biblical monotheism.

Hence, theology as God-talk or God's talk is not necessarily the universally valid starting point, or the direct object, or the only basis, of interreligious collaboration in the Third World. But liberation is. Soteriology is the foundation of theology. Regrettably, the contemporary theologies of religions (with Christ pitted *against* religions or niched *within* them) are devoid of any Third World perspective: they take off from textual accounts of non-Christian religiousness and ignore the historical fact that a religion's micro-ethical concern for self-purification of individuals ("cultural revolution") is often projected onto the macro-ethical level of socio-political catharsis ("structural revolution"). This is true even with those religions that are academically dismissed as "world-denying" or escapist. Equally glossed over are the many explosive liberation myths that, in their symbolic enactments—such as dance and drama, song and ritual, parable and poetry—store the seeds of revolution in the heart of a people. Should not, then, a Third World theology of religions necessarily have a unitary perception of religion and revolution?

I submit that the religious instinct should be defined as a revolutionary urge, a psycho-social impulse, to generate a new humanity. It is none other than the piercing thrust of evolution in its self-conscious state, the human version of nature's thirst for higher forms of life. The religious quest, in other words, is an irresistible drive to *humanize* what has merely been *hominized*. As in the biosphere, where it can end up in blind alleys, so also in the *noosphere*, this evolutionary upsurge can be sidetracked to regressive states of inertia. Revolution could turn reactionary religion irreligious. But the foundation of a Third World theology of religions remains unshaken—namely, that it is this revolutionary impulse that constitutes, and therefore defines, the essence of *homo religiosus*.

This unified view of revolution, religion, and cosmic evolution imparts a Third World dimension to the understanding of technology and the allied concepts of "progress" and "modernization," and consequently lifts the whole debate on inculturation to another plane.

2. Technology is the immediate and inevitable consequence of noogenesis or hominization. The human mind, as it emerges from the biosphere, demands more sensitive organs of perception (senses) and more effective means of movement (limbs), which the body does not provide physiologically. For the mind is capable of extending the brain, the senses, and the limbs of the body by organizing external matter into sensitized and mechanized tools of knowledge and action. Technology, to be sure, is the art (*techne*) of expanding human presence and activity into space and time cognitively and conatively in order to further the psycho-social evolution of humankind. Being the natural accompaniment of hominization, however, technology too can accept or escape the impact of humanization that issues from the revolutionary upsurge of religiousness. Let me therefore recall, with parenthetical explicitations, the concept of technology I earlier proposed to the Ecumenical Association of Third Word Theologians:

> Technology is a [humanly] induced cosmic process, which is a conscious [i.e., self-reflective] continuation of [infrahuman] biological evolution and, like the latter [i.e., like biological evolution], becomes humanized [i.e., liberative] only by its metacosmic orientation [i.e., by the revolutionary thrust of religion toward ever nobler levels of human existence].[68]

If, then, the law of evolution has prescribed in the book of nature the revolutionary imperative to humanize technology through religion, then a dehumanized technocracy is indeed a reversal of the evolutionary trajectory, a cosmological disaster, an irreligious undevelopment, though boorishly advertised in Asian countries as "international culture," modernization, and progress—if not also as preevangelization!

What dehumanizes technology is the sin of acquisitiveness organized into a socio-economic order of human relationships, a distorted cosmology that invariably fosters what Marx calls "the antagonism between man and nature." In that system, technology alienates its inseparable human partner, of whom it was meant to be the cosmic extension; it desecrates the *cosmic religiousness* of the peasant masses with the transfer of biospheric pollution from industrialized countries to the Third World, and with its acquired (not innate) propensity to pillage nature in order to produce the weapons of cosmic holocaust.[69] It deflects the metacosmic orientation of nature and culture with a secularism that eclipses the "beyond" from the "now," and consequently engenders in the human heart a pathological obsession with cosmic need, or "consumerism," as it is known in the cultures that first produced it. Then "modernization" and "progress" *must* imply the overthrow of this regressive but all-persuasive system in favor of a new order of human relationships wherein technology is not so much "in control of" nature as "in harmony with" its inborn thirst for humanization—that is to say, with the revolutionary dictates of religion itself.[70]

Sexism, a sensitive issue in most religions, cannot be divorced from our discourse on technology and civilization, for there is an intimate correspondence between the anthropo-cosmic harmony advocated here and the androgynous mutuality that it presumes. If nature is an exclusively feminine symbol and if the metacosmic beyond, which is the redemptive consummation of the cosmic processes, is made to wear a masculine mask, then of course the religious enterprise of humanizing nature, civilizing technology, and divinizing the human amounts to a masculine absorption of the feminine. Woman will be the last thing to be civilized by man, says George Meredith scornfully; and also vice versa, corrects Theodore Reik.[71]

The task of humanizing nature, which is both masculine and feminine, is founded on the reciprocal activity of men and women civilizing each other. In this area, the revolutionary impulse of all religions—save that of *some* tribal societies and *one* tiny vein in Hinduism—is ruthlessly curbed. Sexism points to an uncivilized area in religion. The new cosmological order that the Third World clamors for includes unhampered feminine participation in religion and revolution.

3. Inculturation, that infelicitous word coined in the West and reminiscent of the reductionist notion of religion running through theology, anthropology, and Marxist ideology, has fortunately come to mean, in present usage, the Christian search for meaning within the *religious* ethos of non-Christian cultures. This is what compelled me to place it in the Christ-of-religions column. In this case, however, the relevant question to be asked is: Into which stream of non-Christian religiousness does Christianity hope to enter—the reactionary or the revolutionary? To allay the liberationists' misgivings about inculturation, one more crucial question has to be raised: Which brand of Christianity seeks to be inculturated, the one framed within a cosmology that is repudiated in the Third World, or the one derived from a Third World hermeneusis of the gospel?

A Third World hermeneusis vivifies the Christian kerygma by recharging the three key words around which it revolves, words now worn out by ideological misuse: *basileia* (the kingdom, or new order), *metanoia* (interior conversion to that order), and *martyrion* (overt commitment to it).

True to our non-Christian religious traditions, we can neither describe nor define the new order but can only boldly strive toward it by the *via negativa*—namely, by negating the present order not only in theory and analysis, but also in the commitment to overthrow it! The future that calls in question the present ever remains the "unnamable" or at least the "unmentioned presupposition" of every true revolution. For the intimate encounter with Ultimate Reality—the core of mysticism—almost overlaps with a profoundly transforming experience of present unreality. The salvific truth dawns as the unmasking of delusion. Being shines in the darkest depths of nonbeing. *Brahma/atman* is reached by piercing through *maya*. Nirvana culminates the pilgrimage of *samsara*. Life is the passage through death. Grace overwhelms where sin abounds. Revolution is born of bondage. Yahweh abides in the *anawim* (the poor). God's saving power erupts from the earth's slaving poor.

Can we touch the one without being touched by the other? Only the victim of the present order is qualified to be its judge and authorized to "proclaim the imminent future"—which is what the kerygma means. *Metanoia*, then, is the disturbance of heart and change of life that such mysticism evokes. It is a religiously motivated desire and decision to move toward the new humanity—a "cultural revolution" in the vocabulary of those who are allergic to the term "religious conversion." *Martyrion* is the concomitant growth of a collective testimony in the communities of converts, a personalized anticipation and a visible guarantee of the new order. Like the supreme martyr, Jesus, they too are the victim-judge of the existing system and the paradigm of the future they announce. This incipient "structural revolution" is known as the church— which is good news to the poor, because the poor by birth and the poor by option constitute it.

Such basic communities are now mushrooming all over the Third World. They are not subservient to the "international culture" of the ministerial church but are shaped by the local religiousness of the poor. As I have argued elsewhere, genuine inculturation is the fruit of ecclesiological revolution, not its seed.[72]

Hence the embarrassing question: Is not the Third World theologian exposed to the same temptation that the Western and westernized anthropologists have succumbed to in their studies of "primitive" cultures? These anthropologists are accused of apocalyptic megalomania in that they claim to possess a secret power of knowing these cultures "empathetically," by reason of "participatory observation," and to have the authority to interpret them to the ignorant West![73]

Inculturationists' enthusiasm for a culture from which they are estranged and liberationists' defense of the poor against those whose culture they happily share, point to a dangerous trend in Third World theology. Should not theology be the explicitation of the theopraxis of these *ecclesiolae* ("little churches") that have appropriated the revolutionary religiousness of the Third World? And should not the writing of this theology be relegated to later redactors? Did not all the sacred scriptures originate in this manner? Is this not the Third World way of doing theology?

9

A Theology of Liberation
in Asian Churches?

VALID THEOLOGY AND THE LOCAL CHURCH:
THE DILEMMA OF ASIAN CATHOLICS

The Roman Instruction on liberation theology recognizes, on biblical grounds, that the phrase "theology of liberation" is "thoroughly *valid*."[1] Liberation—if one may interpret the Roman document—is the contemporary equivalent of the classic theological formula, *economia salutis* (the order of redemption), which is the aspiration of all human beings and the intended goal of all religions. So understood, liberation is the *sole* concern of Christ and his church. Theology is none other than the attempt on the part of the church to spell out this concern in theory and practice, as the Ratzinger document seems to suggest.[2] Does this not mean that the term "theology of liberation" is biblically valid because it is tautological as there cannot be a nonliberational theology? For is it not "liberation" that ultimately determines the validity of any theology? I can begin this chapter, therefore, with agreement on the sign by which a "valid" theology is recognized—namely, a theology is valid if it *originates, develops,* and *culminates* in the praxis/process of liberation.

This argument implies another more significant truth not mentioned in the Roman Instruction—namely, that the same praxis of liberation that makes a theology valid also creates the indigenous identity of the local church that co-originates with that theology. The genesis of a liberation theology overlaps with the genesis of an authentically local church. That is to say, a liberation theology begins to be formulated only when a given Christian community begins to be drawn into a local people's struggle for *full humanity* and through that struggle begins to sink its roots into the life and culture of these people, most of whom are non-Christians. This is why I insist that inculturation and liberation, rightly understood, are two names for the same process!

It is an ecclesiological heresy, therefore, to suppose that a church becomes asianized when the white faces in the Asian episcopate are gradually replaced by black, brown, and yellow ones! An indigenous clergy is not necessarily a sign of an indigenous church! What makes an Asian Christian community

A lecture given at the Fifth International Theological Symposium held at Sophia University, Tokyo, Dec. 1985. First published in *Japan Missionary Bulletin,* 40 (1986) 165-79.

truly indigenous or "local" is its active and risky involvement with Asia's cultural history, which is *now* being shaped by its largely non-Christian majority. Thus, a valid theology of liberation in Asia is born first as a *formula of life,* reflecting an ecclesial praxis of liberation continually internalized by being symbolically reenacted in the liturgy, before it is shaped gradually into a *confessional formula.*

This process is now taking place germinally in the "basic *human* communities" (with Christian and non-Christian membership) emerging on the periphery of the official churches. Therein, the authentically *local* churches of Asia and the *valid* Asian theologies of liberation have already been conceived as twins in the same womb of praxis.

This observation is not true of the official churches. We cannot claim to possess officially any *valid* Asian theology of liberation: the majority of the local churches *in* Asia are not yet local churches *of* Asia. They are extensions of Euro-American local churches *in* Asia. That is why we Catholics who are no more than members of the Asian branch of Rome have no official theology except the *local theology of the local church of Rome.*

By this last phrase, I certainly do not refer to the content of the dogmas of the Roman communion, but to the theological idiom that Rome has evolved from its Christian beginnings, the conceptual framework that supports the practical wisdom, theoretical norms, and pastoral directives emanating from the policy-makers of the Roman church—such as the Ratzinger Instruction on liberation theology and all forms of theologizing that go on within that scheme in the Western patriarchate.

This Roman theology, I readily grant, is a *valid* theology—that is to say, a "liberation theology" in its own right. It has, from its inception, spelled out the what and the how of liberation (= redemption = salvation = coming of the kingdom, etc.) in terms of a distinctively Roman experience. This is how any theology is born.

In this regard, however, I am compelled to make a strange observation: Catholics in the *non-Semitic cultures of Asia* are bound to experience a connaturality, an inner affinity, and a profound empathy vis-à-vis the Roman experience of "liberation" and the Roman articulation of that experience (as will be demonstrated in the next section of this chapter). Hence, there is a strong possibility that even the "indigenized" churches of the future, at least in the non-Semitic sector of Asia, will continue to uphold an Asian version of the Roman perception of liberation.

There are at least two reasons for saying this.

The first reason has already been alluded to: we Asian Catholics have been molded in heart and mind, in doctrine and worship, by the local theology of Rome for four centuries and longer. We have known no other theology since the time we began to breathe as Catholics. It has therefore become *our* sacrosanct tradition, *our* authoritative past, *our* norm of orthodoxy.

The second reason is more important and forms the backbone of the thesis I present here. The gnostic or non-Semitic religions of Asia, such as Hinduism, Buddhism, Jainism, and Taoism, which permeate the popular religiousness and the local cultures of south, southeastern, and far-Eastern Asia, seem to concur with the Roman view of liberation. Thus, if the Asian churches seek to be "inculturated" in and through the religiousness of Asia in the southern and eastern regions, then the Roman view of liberation will continue to be upheld *in toto* as it has always been in the past.

It is therefore our duty to persuade theologians and church leaders not to ignore the following two important facts: one relating to Asian reality, the other directly pertaining to Asian theology.

As regards the first, we should remember that Asian reality cannot be reduced to the great religions, especially to their higher (metacosmic) forms, notwithstanding their decisive influence on our continent. We must pay equal attention to the (cosmic) *religiousness of Asia's poor*, which has its own dynamics (see "The Biblical Perspective: The Messianic Role of the Masses," below). Moreover, I repeat here what I have always held, that the Asian reality is an interplay of *religiousness and poverty*.[3] Both elements have to be taken in their interrelationship. Hence, liberation of the poor, their psycho-spiritual and socio-political emancipation from that which keeps them poor, is an essential concern in an Asian theology. Therefore, the indigenization of the Asian church can never take place if only one sector of Asian reality—that is, only the metacosmic religiousness—is taken seriously. The *religious-ness* of the poor and the *poverty* of the religious masses *together* con-stitute the complex structure of Asian reality that is the matrix of an Asian theology.

The second fact is that Asian religiousness includes also a *Semitic approach* to human liberation, unambiguously set forth in the Bible, especially in the Jewish scriptures and the Synoptics of the New Testament. It is this biblical soteriology that the Latin American theologians have discovered for us anew thanks to their *reditus ad fontes* ("return to the sources") and their immersion in the peoples' poverty, which is the focus of their biblical hermeneusis. It is a source of revelation; it is God's word; it is our authoritative past as well as our norm of orthodoxy for the present. Significantly, it is also a *religious* experi-ence of liberation expressed in a *thoroughly Asian* idiom.

Do we, then, have two competing models of liberation in Asia: on the one hand, that of gnostic religions that seem to agree with the Roman view, and on the other, the biblical model that Latin Americans advocate? How can they both be *valid* theologies if they are contradictory? Or, rather, are they comple-mentary? In other words, should we regard them as optional alternatives, or do they both together constitute the norm of orthodoxy? On the other hand, each seems to resonate with the Asian aspiration for liberation—the one with the gnostic ideal, the other with the Semitic. Hence, I ask: Is this conflict real or apparent? If real, is there a way out?

I foresee that these questions can be wrongly formulated in the Asian church to the detriment of its own theological creativity. The opposition between the two models of liberation, the Roman and the biblical, could be too naively equated with the age-old tension between (the Roman theological) *tradition* and the (revelation of the) *scriptures*; or perhaps between the (Roman) *magiste-*

rium and the (Latin American) *theologians;* or, more frustratingly, between a "theology of *inculturation*" in terms of Asian religiousness (which apparently agrees with the Roman perception of liberation) and a "theology of *liberation*" responding to the poverty and oppression of the Asian masses (being a "biblical" theology articulated by Latin Americans).

My experience with regard to such controversies in the recent past[4] tells me that this species of reductionism should be immediately detected and quickly removed from the visual range of Asian theologians and church leaders. Hence, I propose here to offer an Asian response to these two models of liberation in terms of the *non-Semitic religious cultures of Asia*. This response itself constitutes, I hope, a method of discerning the locus and the method of a liberation theology in our continent.

ROMAN CHRISTIANITY AND THE STOIC PERCEPTION OF "LIBERATION"

The common meeting point between gnostic soteriologies (or Eastern paths of liberation) and the Roman view of salvation is *stoicism*, the noblest of "pagan" ethics and the ideological framework that Christianity absorbed in its early infancy. It bears some affinity with certain currents of spirituality in the East. The process seems to have started as early as the pastoral instructions of the Apostles, though it cannot be noticed in the preaching of Jesus. As the Mediterranean church grew into the Greco-Roman world (which thrived on a slave economy), it entered the ethos of a stoic spirituality, which served it as an apt vehicle of inculturation. Stoicism had an enduring impact on its life and thought. It still has.

According to the stoic anthropology, the human person was not Aristotle's *zoon politikon,* a socio-political animal, but a *zoon koinonikon*, a being in spiritual communion with the whole of humanity. Stoic concern was directed toward peace and harmony at all cost rather than peace and harmony through conflict. This approach was concretely manifested in the *pax romana*, the Roman commonwealth that kept diverse nations and cultures together, minimizing confrontations. Indeed, the Roman church continues the *pax romana* tradition admirably well in what is proverbially known as Vatican diplomacy, and in particular in the exercise of the Petrine office, that special mission entrusted to it of keeping the peace of Christ (*pax christiana*) among the diverse churches in the East and in the West.

On the other hand, the elimination of the unjust socio-political stratification of society in terms of *race, class*, and *sex* could have made sense to the *zoon politikon*, but not to a *zoon koinonikon* with its tendency to *transcend* such social differences spiritually. This tendency more or less continues as the theological mood in the church of Rome even today, and seems exactly what the gnostic religions of Asia want to encourage. This can be demonstrated by the following three observations.

1. First of all, the stoic ideal of liberation was the *interior* emancipation of

the human person from the *interior* bonds of spiritual slavery rather than release from external social structures of enslavement. Thus, for instance, the institution of slavery was taken for granted in the Greco-Roman economic system in much the same way that some Asian cultures take for granted or at least tolerate such social evils as the caste system, domestic servants, and bonded labor.

Inasmuch as the idea of a radical structural change did not seem to enter the mind of the stoics, even the individual emancipation of slaves would appear to be a meaningless exercise, because such manumitted slaves invariably ended up in the spiritually enslaving culture of Greco-Roman society. Hence, many a stoic (e.g. Epictetus) would prefer to see a slave become spiritually free than win legal freedom, because social emancipation did not necessarily exclude internal slavery![5]

Note that this stoic view is valid only when structural change is not possible or not considered. The Roman view today is the same. The idea of "sin" is defined primarily in terms of interior slavery.[6] But the Roman instruction admits the reality of unjust social structures, which it considers to be "consequences" of sin, so that their elimination, though desirable, is not a substitute for the elimination of "sin." Sin here is primarily defined in terms of personal spiritual slavery. This is the main thrust of the Roman argument against the allegedly false brands of liberation theology. It is a position that would square with what Asian religions teach. It certainly is a step more Christian than the original stoic view, which did not sufficiently recognize social sin or structural evil as something that needed to be eliminated.

It is true, however, that the social encyclicals of recent popes have introduced variations to the traditional theological mood of Rome. These encyclicals (significantly, written after Karl Marx) not only contain strong condemnations of unjust social structures, but they also impose on the human/Christian conscience the *obligation* or the evangelical imperative to change inhuman social structures. Yet, Paul VI, the boldest of the modern popes as far as social teachings are concerned, made it clear to the Latin American bishops, at their fifteenth annual general meeting of CELAM held in Rome, that "liberation" means (only) redemption from "sin" and "death." On the same day (Nov. 3, 1974) at the noonday Angelus, he openly dissociated himself and the church from the (presumably Marxist) use of the term "liberation" as a synonym for the process of social emancipation. Instead, he is said to have selected deliberately such words as "true liberty," "authentic justice," "social involvement," and the like, to describe the human activity directed toward a change of sinful structures of society.[7]

2. This position can be traced back to the apostolic writings where another related feature, patent in the contemporary Roman view, begins to germinate. In Galatians 3:28 and parallels, Paul presents the Christian ideal almost in the categories of the stoic (*koinonikon*), in that he advocates a kind of spiritual transcendence of what we today would recognize as *race* (Jew vs. gentile), *class* (slave vs. free), and *sex* (male vs. female); that is to say, a transcendence of such

social divisions *en Christo-Iésou*—that is, in terms of the new belief system of the Christian *koinonia*, the communion of saints. But in actual day-to-day practice, social inequalities were not structurally eliminated even among Christian converts.[8] What mattered was not institutional change with regard to these three societal categories—race, class, and sex (a type of social transformation that was beyond the power of a minority group such as the Christians were). What really mattered was the new Christian way of living and loving within the given, structurally unchangeable division of society (1 Cor. 7:20–24; Col. 3:11, 22; 4:1; Eph. 6:5–9; 1 Tim.6:1; 1 Peter 2:18–20).

According to these apostolic exhortations, Christian wives must obey their husbands and Christian slaves their masters, even the cruel ones; Christian husbands are, of course, exhorted to love their wives, Christian masters their slaves. And so on. Obviously, in the course of time, Christianity brought within that structure a mitigation of social antagonisms.

The same observation can be made with regard to sexist discrimination illustrated in the Roman canonists' attitude to the phenomenon of prostitution; the elimination of this inhuman institution was never their desired goal, but a "Christian" (?) understanding of it was![9]

This is precisely what many of the great religions in Asia have achieved in the cultures they entered. For instance, Buddhism in Sri Lanka absorbed a certain caste-consciousness even into one of its monastic orders, but it has brought some degree of mitigation and reduction of conflicts, though not yet its total elimination, in the Buddhist society of today. It is also a fact that among Buddhists, caste is completely eliminated in places of worship, unlike in Hindu societies and in some Christian communities in Sri Lanka! The process of assimilating social divisions and gradually modifying them (the "assumption-elevation" technique, as it might be called) is the dialectical method of social transformation preferred in Asia. Thus De Nobili, in adopting this method in the case of castes in Madurai,[10] proved himself at once Roman and Asian. The discrimination against women has been softened in the course of centuries through a similar process.

The Roman experience would be quite an acceptable model in our local churches for yet another reason: like the early diaspora churches, we too are *minorities* quite powerless before the unjust institutions of human society. The prophetic role of a minority Christian group in the non-Christian milieu of the Greco-Roman culture seemed to be, not that of denouncing unjust structures, much less of advocating their complete overthrow, but of witnessing to Christian love within such structures, or at least (as in the ancient church of Jerusalem) to produce an ideal community where such structures do not operate. This is not different from the present position of the Roman church and seems also to be the more acceptable "praxis of liberation" that most theologians and church leaders of Asia would readily welcome, for it also coincides with the tenets of all great non-Semitic religions.

Is this policy correct? Perhaps it is, but it is very inadequate, as we shall see. Suffice it to say here that even if this policy is valid as a temporary, stopgap measure in the hands of the Christian minority churches of Asia, much more is expected of Latin America, the most "Christian" among the three continents that mainly constitute the Third World. Hence, if there is more institutional injustice there than elsewhere, the church must be failing in its own missionary and evangelical vocation—namely, that of becoming a sacrament of the kingdom before the other poor nations. A massive Christian *effort* of an organized kind meant to counteract the institutionalized order of mammon is, indeed, a liberational praxis that the Latin American church cannot regard as optional. In this sense, the Nicaraguan Revolution was a great Christian event in Latin American society. The Philippines, the one and only Christian nation in Asia, has a similar obligation toward other Asian nations and toward the diaspora churches in our continent.

3. My third observation is that there are two models of *liberated persons* (at least one of which originated in stoicism), which are now part and parcel of Catholicism and are not without parallels in the religious traditions of the non-Semitic East. Because this third observation is the most significant for an Asian theologian concerned with liberation, I turn now to a lengthier treatment of it.

THE ELITIST CONCEPT OF THE "LIBERATED PERSON"

I must point out that the stoicism that entered the bloodstream of Catholicism was not the spirituality of the slave and the poor classes, but that of the highbrow philosophy of the elite. Many nobles and administrators of the Roman empire were guided by its ethics. Emperor Marcus Aurelius, whose *Meditations* appealed to generations of Roman Christians, was one of them.

Christianity appropriated the stoic ethics in the measure that it gradually ceased to be the religion of a persecuted people and became acceptable among the aristocracy. Long before the Constantinian era, Christianity climbed the social ladder thanks to marriages of Christian women with pagan nobles and thanks to the emergence of a "nobility of service" (parallel to the nobility of lineage) that gave Christians an entry into the higher administrative echelons of Roman society. This was the process by which Christianity became respectable in Rome.[11] It was also the way Christianity crystalized the stoic approach to social problems, which had already begun in the pastoral exhortations of Paul and his collaborators.

As an aristocratic spirituality, stoicism also enshrined the belief that the wise man or philosopher was always the fully *human* person who, therefore, was called to guide commoners—the hoi polloi—who were only potentially human.[12] Despite the Pauline doctrine of the mystical body of Christ, and the Christian communism of the church of Jerusalem, there began to grow a two-tiered spirituality of elite and commoners among Christians. Note also that the comfortable and elitist life of "pagan" Rome's flamens and especially of the vestal virgins offered the church a model of celibate elitism that was not necessarily tied to absolute poverty or renunciation of power and prestige! There arose a class of wise and learned men and women who had no faith in the redemptive power of the poor or in the spiritual capabilities of the common people.

Aristocratized in the process of being christianized, the church of Rome soon produced two symbols of spiritual liberation: the first took inspiration from the Roman pagan idea of *otium* or "holy leisure." The second was also a borrowed idea: the "Eastern" model of the "desert."[13] And I repeat, both these models have their parallels in Asian religions.

The *otium* or comfortable retirement in faraway estates or villas was a frequent practice of nobles and senators (both pagan and Christian) who wished to give more time to reflection on their own lives, writing memoirs or reediting manuscripts. One historian thinks that "the first monasteries in the West were 'lay monasteries' of sensitive pagans."[14] Augustine, too, is said to have looked upon his own retirement to Cassiciacum as *Christianae vitae otium.*[15] The aim was to indulge in a kind of "philosophical life."

This image of the pagan/Christian philosopher reflecting and writing about the ultimate concerns of life in comfortable retirement continues in the lifestyle of contemporary theologians in most Asian seminaries. As members of the "leisure class" with plenty of time for academic speculation on religious matters, they are not the type to be radically committed to social and interpersonal justice, or inclined to identify themselves with the poorer classes on whose "surplus" they probably live. The feudal spirit that still permeates Asian societies and the monarchico-aristocratic structure of the presbyterian/episcopal institution of the Roman church hardly discourages theologians from adopting this social model.

This species of spiritual/intellectual elitism was not without its own counterpart in Eastern religions. For instance, the Chinese Mandarin (the cultured and wise administrator-thinker that confucianism produced) and the Indian Brahmin (the high-caste spiritual leader who sat on the top of the social pyramid to guide caste-ridden Hindu society) were precisely the two models that Matteo Ricci in Beijing and De Nobili in Madurai found worthy of imitation in the process of what we call "inculturation" today, but known in their times as "adaptation."

De Nobili—himself a member of the Roman nobility—cited the early Roman praxis as a precedent to justify his method to ecclesiastical authorities. In his famous manifesto, he modestly advertised his own aristocratic lineage, presumably to gain spiritual authority and social acceptance in the Hindu hierocracy. De Nobili, it is certainly true, took the guise of a renouncer, a *sannyasi*, with various ascetical practices proper to it, thus shunning the *otium* model; yet he was no ordinary renouncer; he was, as he claimed, a *"Brahmin sannyasi,"* an ascetic of the highest social rank. If the conversion of a people and its culture to the Roman church is a criterion of missionary success, then De Nobili's method of evangelizing the Indian Brahmins was indisputably successful, the Roman Instruction of 1659 notwithstanding.[16]

But India has changed since then; so have China and most countries of Asia. Now that Marxism has become an all-pervasive ideology and a quasi religion in vast stretches of Asia—something that Latin America has not yet experienced—there seems to be an inversion of values. In the eyes of many an enlightened "proletariat," it is the elite of the leisure class including religious leaders who need to be liberated, and this liberation can be achieved only in and through the *self-redemptive action of the masses*, the commoners, the hoi polloi, the poor, the oppressed, who are thought to be invested with a messianic mission for the total liberation of humankind.

Fortunately, *otium* is not the only paradigm of liberation that Roman Christianity has produced. Thanks to the winds of spiritual emancipation that blew from outside the Christian world, there came to be established an alternative image of liberation: the *desert*. In fact, it was the desert fathers who laid a solid foundation for the tradition of *organized* monasticism that gained recognition in the Roman church, though it is true that the germinal idea of the desert experience and the practice of renunciation was thoroughly biblical and Christian in content and inspiration. It had already been anticipated in circles of consecrated virgins in the apostolic and postapostolic church and in other fraternities of nonhermetic origin in later centuries.

The desert model was also anticipated in the pre-Christian era among Hellenistic philosophers of various schools (Stoics, Cynics, Neo-Pythagoreans, Neo-Platonists, and others), who in their search for wisdom or philosophy opted to be poor—that is, to free themselves from worldly concerns and possessions. Origen and St. Jerome thought of them as anticipators of Jesus' own poverty, and regarded the renunciation of possessions as a condition for acquiring "a *state* of spiritual perfection" (thus misinterpreting— Hellenistically—the call narrative in Matt. 19:21).[17] This nonbiblical concept of voluntary poverty, common to the gnostic religions both of the East and of the Hellenistic West, is best exemplified in Christian Rome's "desert movement," which we are concerned with here.

The "desert" during the first centuries of the Christian era was not only a positive symbol of an earnest *search for God* in solitude and in the company of nature, but also a negative symbol of *social protest* against the worldly values that infected the contemporaneous church and society. Both of these elements together constitute the élan of the desert movement.

Asia experienced this phenomenon at least nine centuries earlier than Rome—in the Gangetic culture of the sixth century before Christ. The corresponding symbol in India at that time (and since then) was the "forest"—the ecological haven to which the urbanized youth of the day took recourse, not only in *search* of the ultimate meaning of life but also in *protest* against a clericalized and ritualized religion, and against the urbanized, unfree, war-ridden society of the times. It was a spiritual search as well as a social protest. Thus arose one of the first historically documented monastic movements not only in Asia, but in the world.

The desert fathers of the Christian West and the forest hermits of the non-Christian East seem to have both formulated for all times two important dimensions of genuine asceticism: (1) *interior liberation* from worldly possessions (material poverty) or at least from greed for possessions (spiritual poverty); and (2) *visible rejection of a society* that is egocentric, acquisitive, power-hungry, and dehumanizing.

It is true that this noble, twofold ideal (sometimes carried to Manichean extremes) succumbed later to the phenomenon of feudalization, almost degenerating to the level of *otium,* the "leisure-class mentality" prevalent even today in large-propertied monasteries both in the Roman world and in Asian cultures. It could also generate an elitist form of spirituality not available or possible for the ordinary person! Yet the renewalist movements that such abuses provoked periodically in the monastic tradition itself always rediscovered and reaffirmed the aforementioned twofold dimension. In biblical language it can be reformulated as (1) the *renunciation* of mammon within one's inner self, a renunciation coinciding with the liberating search for God, and (2) the indirect and silent *denunciation* of a world order built on mammonic values. The monastic, then, is a sacrament of what is possible and, at various levels, obligatory for all, rather than a symbol of an elitist spirituality.

According to this model of the liberated person, both Roman Christianity and the non-Christian East succeed in making the image of the philosopher and the sage coincide with that of a poor person, a mendicant. Two principal dimensions of monastic life—namely, the personal rejection of wealth-accumulation or mammon as anti-God, and the establishment of a socially recognizable sign of that rejection—constitute the *starting point* of a liberation theology in Asia. It is a starting point based on a principle revealed in all religions, biblical and nonbiblical: that God or the Liberative Agent is irreconcilably opposed to mammon or wealth-accumulation, the source of human enslavement. The "desert" in the Roman experience and the "forest" in the Indian correspond to the biblical symbol of the wilderness, the place where God and mammon compete for our allegiance.[18]

But there is another axiom revealed *only* in the Bible, specific *only* to the Christian faith and *totally absent in all non-Semitic religions* but explosively *true in the context of Marxist analysis*: that this same God has made a defense pact—a covenant—with the poor against the agents of mammon, so that the struggle of the poor for their liberation coincides with God's own salvific action. The stoicism of pagan Rome (ideologically operative in current Roman theology) and the asceticism of Eastern monks (Asia's social symbol of liberation) offer no *explicit teaching* on the matter. But the theological and pastoral consequences of this biblical axiom determine in concrete the specific contribution of Christians in Asia. This, in my opinion, is the biblical principle that Latin Americans have discovered for us. It has been misunderstood in Rome and in Asia as an ideological borrowing from Marx.

To this, then, we must now turn our attention.

THE BIBLICAL PERSPECTIVE: THE MESSIANIC ROLE OF THE MASSES

No liberation theology can claim to be rooted in the word of God if it does not hold together the two biblical axioms mentioned above: (1) the irreconcilable antagonism between *God and mammon*, and (2) the irrevocable covenant between *God and the poor* (i.e., a defense pact against their common enemy: mammon).

As already observed, the first axiom is a universal spiritual dogma that defines the very core of practically all religions of Asia and manifests itself symbolically in the figure of the *monk/nun* or any of its many equivalents. This universal symbol of *opted poverty* can never be dispensed with in any liberational action or speculation in our continent, because it is the symbol by which our cultures have, for centuries, affirmed (1) not only that the Absolute alone is the ultimate source and the intimate moment of liberation, but (2) also that the cult of mammon or the enthronement of capital (profit-accumulation) is not merely *not* the guarantee of human liberation but is certainly the very negation of that liberation. Thus the negation of this negation—that is to say, the open repudiation (not necessarily the overthrow)—of any order of society based on a cult of mammon is an essential ingredient of Asian religiousness as symbolized in the monastic ideal of *voluntary poverty*.

In fact, Buddhism stands out in bold relief among the gnostic religions in making this important deduction from the first axiom. Concealed beneath the mythical language of the *Aggañña Sutta, Cakkavatti-Sīhnāda-Suttanta,* and the *Kūṭanāda Suttanta,* taken together, is the Buddha's explosive social message: that it is *taṇhā*—the acquisitive tendency, the accumulative instinct in the human heart—that generates all social evil; that it lays the foundation for the vicious idea of private property in place of the saner practice of common ownership. It thus brings about class divisions and absolute poverty, which lead to all types of human misery and have repercussions on the cosmos itself, affecting the quality of life and reducing the lifespan of humankind.[19] Amid such a society, the monastic community ideally composed of greedless men and women presents itself as an eschatological community that symbolizes and even anticipates what *could* be everybody's future.

This explains the effectiveness of the already mushrooming *basic human communities* with Christian and non-Christian membership, which give testimony to this universal dogma of spirituality: the God-mammon antinomy. Christian members would describe such communities as "sacraments" of the kingdom or social embodiments of the Beatitudes. Many such ashrams and their equivalents by their practice of voluntary poverty (rejection of mammon) remain the only dream of a new social order.

However, this experiment, in most instances, used the *via negativa* proper to the Oriental mentality, for it is a way of saying what human liberation *is*, by showing what it is *not*. The liberated human community is clearly shown *not* to be the present one, for the liberated community is one in which greed is *not* organized into principalities and powers. Such prophetic communities are the founders of the not-yet-discovered liberation theology in Asia, for they are the seeds of the not-yet-developed local churches of Asia.

But positive action toward the reconstruction of a new order of love (or kingdom of God)—action whose final result only *approximates* the ideal that everyone dreams of (the ideal in itself is of course a gratuitous gift dawning from the other side of our human horizon)—has not been clearly embarked on wherever the second axiom—God's partiality to the poor—has not been given due recognition in one's spirituality.

For instance, many gnostics of the Greco-Roman culture practiced poverty as a condition for attaining wisdom and perfection, and at times were ostentatious in their renunciation; their *voluntary poverty* was not motivated by any form of solidarity with those condemned to *forced poverty*. Hence, the "well-known insensitivity of impecunious philosophers to the misery of the needy"[20] contrasts sharply with the Christian praxis of the Roman church, which rose above the stoics' indifference to the poor. This is because the fathers of the church and the great founders of monastic communities kept the church from forgetting that it is in the poor that Christ seeks to be ministered to. Thus, the Roman church has gone a step further than the pagan ascetics whenever it was guided by the gospel of Jesus.

However, there is still a third step we are forced to take in our understanding of the poor when the second axiom is taken seriously. It is not enough to consider the poor passively as the sacramental recipients of our ministry, as if their function in life were merely to help us, the rich, to save our souls by our retaining them as perpetual objects of our compassion. That would be to take Matthew 25:31ff. out of the general context of the gospel teaching on the role of the poor in the coming of the kingdom, a teaching in continuation, albeit in a more subdued tone, with the more forceful doctrine contained in the Jewish scriptures. The poor must be seen as *those through whom God shapes our salvation history*. This doctrine has been very clearly set forth in the context of the current controversy between Rome and Latin American theologians by the Indian biblical scholar George Soares-Prabhu, S.J.[21] After a meticulous study of the Jewish scriptures and New Testament vis-à-vis this question, he comes to these three conclusions:

1. The poor in the Bible form a *sociological* group whose identity is defined not by their religious attitude but by their sociological situation. [In other words, we are not dealing merely with a species of "spiritual" poverty, a sort of stoic detachment from material things or attachment to God, but of material poverty.]
2. The poor in the Bible are also a *dialectical* group whose situation is determined by antagonistic groups standing over and against them.
3. The poor in the Bible are a *dynamic* group who are not the passive victims of history but those through whom God shapes his history.[22]

If there is some similarity between these three biblical tenets and Marxist theory, which sees the poor (proletariat) as a social class at once victim and creator of human history, we can only say that the Bible could not have borrowed it from Marx! Yet Soares-Prabhu makes this pertinent observation, which is worth quoting in full:

Poverty in the Bible is indeed primarily a sociological category but it is not to be defined in purely economic, much less in Marxist, terms (non-ownership of the means of production). Biblical poverty has a broader sociological and even a *religious meaning*. The poor in the Bible are an oppressed group in conflict, but it is doubtful whether their conflict can be usefully described as a class struggle. Factors other than the need to control the means of production or to secure economic betterment enter into it, and give it a different colour. The poor in the Bible aspire after a free, fraternal, and non-exploitative community which does indeed call to mind the classless society of Karl Marx. But the Bible goes beyond Marx's classless society in its affirmation of a *religious basis for social justice*. The "new heavens and the new earth" will be "full of the knowledge of the Lord as the waters cover the sea" (Isa. 11:9; 65:25); and in the New Jerusalem God Himself will dwell with humankind and they will be His people and He will be with them (Rev. 21:3-4).[23]

In the light of this observation, we can now review the various perceptions of liberation—namely, (1) that of pagan Rome, (2) of Christian Rome, (3) of non-Christian Asia, and (4) of Marxism, and thus discover what is specific to the biblical faith.

The stoic perception, which is the ideological substratum of Roman theology, sees liberation primarily as spiritual/personal/interior. It does, however, tolerate an individual's search for freedom from external social structures that are oppressive—as exemplified in the case of slavery. But it does not envisage any radical change of social structures.

The Roman theology that christianized stoic ethics goes further. It clearly mitigates, with Christian love, social antagonisms between the various divisions of society. Moreover, it also earnestly pleads for change of evil social structures. But it clearly upholds that such structural change is secondary to and a consequence of interior spiritual liberation achieved through love. In this matter, "Buddhism of the texts," as shown above, takes a similar stand.

The minimal view commonly attributed to Marxists restricts liberation to a class struggle of the poor (= proletariat) aimed at socio-economic justice (beginning with common ownership of the means of production and ending up, it is hoped, in a classless and stateless society).

In contrast to these three positions, biblical revelation seems to advocate a unitary perception of all these aspects of liberation so that it admits a mutuality in dyads—personal/social, spiritual/material, internal/structural—whenever these are predicated of "sin" and "liberation from sin."

Secondly, liberation in the Bible is a *religious experience of the poor*, for what liberates is the redeeming love of God, and the final fruit of liberation is the saving knowledge of God! Biblical liberation is *more* than class struggle. It is the God-encounter of the poor, the poor by choice (the renouncers) and the poor by circumstances (the *anawim* of Yahweh).

Thirdly, the liberation that the Bible speaks of is a *joint venture of God and the people (poor) covenanted into one indivisible Saving Reality.* Human efforts and divine initiatives merge into one liberating enterprise. Yet even the highest human achievement either in the personal perfection of the individual (as in traditional spiritualities) or in the collective perfection of a social group (as in a liberation spirituality) does not even approach the final glory, which remains a grace, a gratuitous gift of God, immeasurable by any human criterion.

Fourthly, it is not merely individuals, but also racial groupings, cultures, peoples, and *nations* that are called to be perfect as the heavenly Father is perfect. But the crucial fact is that nations are judged by their *victims,* Christ himself being the "victim-judge" of nations (Matt. 25:31ff.). Hence, the missionary mandate to make "disciples of all nations" is an invitation to all minority churches of Asia to join in the process of educating the nations to fear the judgments of the victims they themselves create!

Such a project is possible in Asia only if we Christians judiciously appropriate the *religiousness of the poor* as our own spirituality, for it is the locus for a theology of liberation in Asia. This is the final thesis I want to explore in this chapter.

ASIAN THEOLOGY AND
THE RELIGIOUSNESS OF THE POOR

"The religiousness of the poor" is an entirely new focus in the theological reflection of the Asian church and can be traced back to the Asian Theological Conference of 1979.[24] There Asian reality was described as an interplay of Asian (mostly non-Christian) *religiousness* and *poverty*. Within five years, some bishops of Asia had assimilated this theme into their pastoral reflection. In fact, in 1985 they took part in exposure-immersion programs that were meant to put them in touch with the religiousness of the poor so that their dream of a "church of the poor" (a recurrent theme in the Federation of Asian Bishops' Conferences [FABC] statements) could be a reality. This was also the theme of the seventh session of the Bishops' Institute for Social Action (BISA VII) in January 1986.

When admitting that religiousness and poverty constitute the Asian reality, we should also remember that the theme "religiousness of the poor" defines, in some way, the leitmotif of the Bible. In making this statement, I am indulging in a specifically Asian reading of the Bible, which is in itself a theological exercise that reveals the dynamics of a liberation praxis in Asia: the discovery, through participation in the lives of others, of the revolutionary potential of their (Christian and non-Christian) religiousness—something that Marxists have not yet discovered.

To be more concrete, the Bible, as we understand it in our Asian context, is the record of a *religious experience* of a "nonpeople" struggling to be a "people," a struggle in which God is an intimate partner. The dozen or more centuries that constitute the history of this people, from the exodus to the beginnings of Christianity, were on the whole a period of humiliations for the Hebrews, except for minor intervals of peace, the longest of which was about a century (1000–900 B.C.). They were almost always subject to the rulers of the "developed" nations around them—the Egyptians, Assyrians, Babylonians, Ptolomies, Greeks, and finally the Romans. What the Bible documents for us is the religious experience (the faith commitment, the spirituality of struggle) that characterized a colonized and exploited people—an excellent paradigm of a God-encounter (that is, liberation) for the Asian poor.

Another factor about the religiousness of this poor nation of Israel was its ability to perceive the norms and principles of a *just society* as set forth in the Sinai covenant, though its fidelity to that ideal was not always exemplary! None of the colonizer nations ever formulated such advanced canons of just government based on human dignity. How could they? It is the poor, the oppressed, the colonized who religiously experience the justice of God and understand God's just demands, for it is to them that the divine opens its heart. The textual religions in Asia need to be revitalized by the people's religion that contains the seed of this revelation, as exemplified by the Buddhist experiment cited below.

There is finally another lesson the Asian poor can learn from the chosen people: there was one "glorious" era when Israel thought it could be a "people" according to the standards of the "advanced" nations. But was it a people in God's eyes? The experiment itself raised this question. The period of the Kings (Saul, David, and Solomon) saw the disastrous consequences of aping the richer nations that did not know Yahweh! Liberation does not mean aping the rich; it means teaching the rich nations the justice of Yahweh.

These are the biblical data that support the insight that the religiousness of the Asian poor (who are largely non-Christian) could be a new source of revelation for the Asian church. The inculturation theologies busy *only* with the philosophical speculations of non-Christian religious texts have to be abandoned in favor of *theological communities* of Christians and non-Christians who form basic human communes with the poor, sharing the common patrimony of a *religiousness* that their (voluntary or forced) *poverty* generates. It is they who will interpret sacred texts in the light of their religious aspiration for freedom.

I have appealed to such communities to study the history of Asian religions in terms of the many liberation movements that, in the past, have imparted to sacred texts a contextual hermeneusis explicitating the implicit liberational currents that flow within such traditional religions. I have also illustrated this by educing examples from south Asian, southeast Asian, and far-Eastern history.[25]

It is heartening to note that in Sri Lanka we have even today a small nucleus of Buddhist monks with no "power," "property," or "prestige" to rely on, but only their poverty to boast of. They are radically committed to the life they share with the poor, thus voicing the systematically silenced protests of the voiceless, including ethnic minorities. The Buddhism that appears in the columns of their explosive periodical *Vinivida* has made a new hermeneusis of textual religion on the basis of the lived experience of the poor. They call themselves the "Humanist Buddhist Monks' Association" and have successfully allowed the demands of history to uncover the hitherto unknown social dynamics of a gnostic religion.

Thus, the limitations of the desert model (two-tiered spirituality, exclusive concern with interior liberation, etc.) are eliminated by a monastic or ascetical life that feeds on the religious (that is, liberative) aspirations of the poor.

This Buddhist experiment is paralleled by many basic *human* communities of Christian and non-Christian poor who reflect together and articulate their hope for a holier future by boldly neutralizing every human obstacle that stands in their way. These symbolic beginnings are forerunners of many such theological communities where the seed of liberation theologies, once sown, will grow to maturity. The written records of the Christian Workers' Fellowship in Sri Lanka are a testimony to these seminal liberation theologies. The bishops who were exposed to these groups in August 1985 were visibly moved and pleasantly surprised by the evangelical boldness of their experiment, the theological depth of their reflections, and the non-Christian contribution to their Christian theology.

We pray that here in Asia this new method of theology will be respected or at least tolerated by those who have the power to frustrate it. The first step in this method is the building up of "kingdom communities" or "basic human communities" wherein Christian and non-Christian members strive together for the dawn of *full humanity*. "Full humanity" is not only the common ideal of their strivings, but also the christological title by which the Christian members of such communities would recognize and confess the One whose disciples they boldly claim to be.

Moreover, the non-Christian context (that is, the religiousness of the Asian poor) imparts an indelible cultural stamp on such communities so as to challenge Christian members to articulate their new (that is, Asian) religious identity. This new Christian identity can be easily detected in the theological language employed in many liturgies celebrated in these "theological communities of the poor."

Regrettably, some of us are misnamed "Asian theologians" when in reality all we do is explicitate this implicit theology and educe the ecclesiological implications of this newly-found Asian Christian identity. In doing so, however, we do articulate a theology of liberation for our continent and simultaneously announce the birth of genuine local churches *of* Asia.

Postscript

Asia's Search for Christ:
A Scriptural Meditation

The general theme of this book is not of my creation. It comes from the pen of an Asian writer known as Matthew Levi. His subject is Asia's search for Christ. In a mythical idiom, he dramatizes an authentically historical fact: that of *Orientals looking westward for an encounter with Christ.* This ever-recurring event is deeply embedded in the Christian memory and is exteriorized ritually on every January 6: the Epiphany—Christ's revelation to Orientals.

Matthew puts it in the form of a three-act tragedy: search, disillusionment, and discovery (Matt. 2:1–12). The whole drama is packed with pithy theological utterances astoundingly contemporary in their implications.

Act I: Search. "We saw his star in the east and have come to do him homage" (Matt. 2:2). Here Matthew has laid the foundation for an Asian theology of religions, which he builds up into a magnificent structure later. In this terse formula, he has compressed at least six theological pointers:

a) A *light* has appeared in the East. Therefore with regard to the process of liberation, the East is not clueless.

b) It was *his* light that they saw. Christ's coming is revealed in the East even before Jerusalem hears about it.

c) They *recognize* it as his light.

d) They recognize it as a *sacramental pointer* to a mystery that entices them to a deeper search; they are not content with the light and so they look for its source.

e) Hence the *long journey* through the deserts and lonely highways. The Orientals do not know any shortcuts; their way is tedious and ascetically demanding!

f) The light leads them *westward,* to a city on a mountain.

Act II: Disillusionment. Now Matthew brings the whole drama to a peak of irony, contrasting the seriousness of the Asian sages with the complacency of God's priests in Jerusalem.

The stage is in total darkness as the curtain rises. The pilgrims grope their way for light.

a) The *light* that shines in the East *is not seen* in the city on the mountain (2:9). Jerusalem is in the dark with regard to the birth of Christ.

From "Contemporary Ecumenism and Asia's Search for Christ," *Teaching All Nations,* 13 (1976) 28-30.

b) It is from the Eastern sages that Jerusalem hears the good news (2:2–3). It is through them that God *reveals* to God's own people in Jerusalem that the divine is present in Christ. It is their inquiry that provokes the priests to read the scriptures for further light (2:4–6).

c) The question that epitomizes the Asian quest is not "Who is he?" or "What is he?" but "*Where* is he?" (2:2a), as if to say, "put us in contact with Christ, not with christology," for *"we have come to do him homage"* (2:2b). What satisfies their thirst is *experience*, not explanations!

d) Herod (who would not hesitate to kill the innocent in a moment of insecurity) and "the whole of Jerusalem" are *perturbed* by the good news (2:3). When Asia's struggle to discover the ultimate source of liberation comes to fruition at the doorstep of the West, with the news, "the Liberator is here," it does not sound like "good tidings" to the establishment, both secular and religious. In such a situation, anything may be resorted to, in order to suppress the imminent liberation (2:16).

e) Neither *God's word* in the Bible nor *God's people* in Jerusalem are the goal of the Asian pilgrimage. But they both are consulted in the course of the quest. They serve the pilgrims of Christ as *sacraments* inviting them to go beyond. In fact the Magi leave the "holy city" in order to find Christ!

f) The final scene: the sages from the East depart *alone!* Jerusalem's priests, custodians of the law, interpreters of revelation, guardians of tradition, and guides of Israel, *would not join the Asians in their search for Christ,* and consequently fail to participate in their discovery (2:12).

Act III: Discovery. The Asians' tedious journey in pursuit of the liberator ends up in a *laborer's hut!* They discover that the light shining in the East radiates from a *rural house!* The liberation of Asia is announced from a *rustic's improvised home.* The *Asian Christ* is found seated on the knees of a *peasant woman, a worker's wife.* And this is the end of the quest! (2:10–11).

Asian wisdom crouches in humility before a villager's son. This is true worship, liturgy supreme: they adore the savior, laying down their gold at the doorstep of his shanty home (2:11).

They return home eastward with the good news. The same providence that guided them to the savior has them bypass Jerusalem, the institutional center of God's people. Its leadership was not available for the Asians in their search for Christ, and, therefore, it is not indispensable for proclaiming him in Asia (2:12).

NOTES

CHAPTER 1

1. See Peter MacCartin, "Theology of Liturgy," *Tjurunga, An Australasian Benedictine Review*, 6 (1974) 93–106; 7 (1974) 67–75; 9 (1975) 89–96; 11 (1976) 59–72.

2. I. Iglesia, "The Contemplative Dimension in the Writings of Pope John Paul II, Introduction," *IGNIS* (Bombay), 11 (1982) 13ff.

3. *God the Future of Man* (New York: Sheed and Ward, 1968), pp. 98–103; emphasis added.

CHAPTER 2

1. See Ludwig Wiedenmann, ed., *Herausgefordert durch die Armen. Dokumente der Oekumenischen Vereinigung von Dritte-Welt-Theologen, 1976–1983* (Freiburg: Herder, 1983).

2. Jon Sobrino, *Christology at the Crossroads* (Maryknoll, N.Y.: Orbis, 1978), p. 93.

3. I. Ellacuría, *Freedom Made Flesh* (Maryknoll, N.Y.: Orbis, 1976), pp. 54–60.

4. Rahner and Duquoc, quoted in Sobrino, *Christology*, p. 97 and p. 141, n. 23.

5. *Tablet* (Oct. 30, 1971), p. 1060.

6. *Epistola XVIII*, nos. 11–12 (PL 16,975).

7. Cf. Stanislaus Lyonnet, *The Meditation on the Two Standards and Its Scriptural Foundation* (in T. A. Burke, Program to Adapt the Spiritual Exercises [Jersey City, N.J.: n.d.]).

8. R. B. Y. Scott and G. Vlastos, eds., *Towards the Christian Revolution*, (London: Gollancz, 1937), p. 104.

9. Leonardo Boff, "Pelos pobres e contra la pobreza," in *Convergencia* (May 1979), pp. 232–37.

10. For quotations, references, and comments, see José Miranda, *Marx and the Bible: A Critique of the Philosophy of Oppression* (Maryknoll, N.Y.: Orbis, 1974), pp. 15–16.

11. Boff, "Pelos pobres," pp. 232–37.

12. Oxford: Pergamon Press, 1978.

13. Juan María Lozano, *Discipleship: Towards an Understanding of Religious Life* (Chicago: Claretian Press, 1980), pp. 173–74.

14. Ibid., p. 177.

15. From the Final Statement, *Dialogue*, 7 (1980) 121.

16. *Acta Apostolicae Sedis*, 62 (1971) 497–526.

CHAPTER 5

1. See A. Luneau, "To Help Dialogue: The Fathers and the Non-Christian Religions," *Bulletin of the Secretariate for Non-Christians* (Vatican City) 3 (1968) 14.

2. For historical background, see chap. 8, below, pp. 88–89, 93–96.

3. In a documentary entitled *The Church—Non-Christians—Monks* (St. Louis, U.S. National Center for Aide Intermonastère, 1982), Abbot Simon Tonini, O.S.B.,

shows that with the increasing exposure of the popes to other religions, their openness grows from mere condenscension to positive and uninhibited admiration.

4. For a theological reflection on this, see chap. 8, below, pp. 83–84.

5. In a careful study of the origin and meaning of the term "inculturation," Francis Clark, S.J. ("Making the Gospel at Home in the Asian Cultures," *Teaching All Nations*, 13 [1976] 131–49), thinks that Fr. J. Masson, S.J., was among the first to introduce the word into contemporary Missiology (p. 149, n. 5).

6. Y. Congar, "Christianity as Faith and Culture," *East Asian Pastoral Review*, (1981), p. 313. This is the English translation of the Italian original, *Evangelizazzione e cultura*, Congresso Internazionale di Missiologia, Oct. 5–12, 1976 (Rome: Pontificia Università Urbaniana, 1976), pp. 83–103. I quote the English translation.

7. See A. Pieris, "Western Christianity and Eastern Religions" (A Theological Reading of Historical Encounters), *Cistercian Studies* (1980) 50–66 and 150–71.

8. As observed by Wolfhart Pannenberg, *Theology and Philosophy of Science* (London: Faber, 1976), p. 10.

9. D. Snellgrove, "Traditional and Doctrinal Interpretation of Buddhahood: An Outline of a 'Theology' of Buddhahood," *Bulletin of the Secretariate for Non-Christians*, 5 (1970) 3–24.

10. Chap. 7, below, p. 85.

11. The reasons for this skepticism are given in chap. 4, above, pp. 38–42.

12. G. Vitanage, "The New Look with a Note: A Comment on Fr. Mervyn Fernando's article on 'Is Adaptation Outmoded?,' " *Quest* (Colombo), 4 (1969) 80–81.

13. Jean Delumeau, "Les Reformes, la protestante et la catholique, ont imposé aux masses la religion de l'élite," extracts from an address given at the Collége de France on Feb. 13, 1975, and published in *Informations Catholiques Internationales*, May 2, 1975, pp. 21ff.

14. For a detailed presentation of this thesis, see chap. 8, below, pp. 98–100, and chap. 7, below, pp. 71–74.

15. For a biblico-theological reflection on this theological method, see chap. 4, above, pp. 45–50.

16. Louis Bouyer, ed., *The History of Christian Spirituality. Part I: The Spirituality of the New Testament and the Fathers* (London: Burns and Oates, 1963), chap. 9.

17. See Reginaldo Gregoire, "Esiste una teologia monastica?" *Inter Fratres* (Rome), 27 (1977) 115–20.

18. Juan María Lozano, *Discipleship: Towards an Understanding of Religious Life* (Chicago: Claretian Press, 1980), pp. 172–78.

19. See *Asian Monastic Conference, Kandy, Sri Lanka*, Aug. 18–24, 1980 (Aide Intermonastère, Vanves, France, 1981), p. 219.

20. The theological method and idiom used in the Asian Theological Consultation (ATC) of 1979 was seriously misunderstood in Rome. The relevant documents are available at the Centre for Religion and Society, 281 Deans Rd., Colombo 10, Sri Lanka.

21. After a long debate on this point (see *Voices from the Third World* (Colombo), vol. 2, no. 1, June 1979) the members of the Ecumenical Association of the Third World Theologians (EATWOT) seem to have agreed that true inculturation and liberation almost converged not only in Asia but in other parts of the Third World. This can be inferred from the Final Statement of the EATWOT fifth conference held in New Delhi, 1981; see V. Fabella and S. Torres, eds., *Irruption of the Third World* (Maryknoll, N.Y.: Orbis 1983), pp. 201–2.

CHAPTER 6

1. For a list of the relevant writings from 1600 to 1965, see K. Baago, *Library of Indian Christian Theology: A Bibliography* (Madras: Christian Literature Society, 1969).

2. For a summary, see R. H. S. Boyd, *An Introduction to Indian Christian Theology* (Madras: Christian Literature Society, 1969); K. Baago, *Pioneers of Indigenous Christianity* (Bangalore: Christian Institute for the Study of Religion and Society, 1969).

3. K. Sivaraman, "Resources in Hindu Morality and Religion," in *Towards World Community: The Colombo Papers*, S. J. Samartha, ed. (Geneva: World Council of Churches, 1975), p. 28.

4. K. N. Jayatilleke, *The Buddhist Attitude to Other Religions* (Colombo: Public Trustee Dept., 1966), p. 16.

5. The most articulate exposition of this thesis in the 1960s was A. T. Van Leeuwen's *Christianity in World History: The Meeting of Faiths of East and West* (London: Edinburgh House Press, 1964). The theory was still circulating in the 1970s; see, e.g., P. Gheddo, *Why is the Third World Poor?* (Maryknoll, N.Y.: Orbis, 1973), pp. 30–37 and passim.

6. See the relevant documents in *Asia's Struggle for Full Humanity*, V. Fabella, ed. (Maryknoll, N.Y.: Orbis, 1980).

7. Ibid., pp. 75–95.

8. See *Voices from the Third World*, Vol. 2, no. 1, June 1979.

9. Matt. 3:13–17 and parallels; Mark 10:38, 39; Luke 12:50. For a theological excursus on this theme, see chap. 4, above, pp. 45–50.

10. See M. R. Spindler, "Recent Indian Studies of the Gospel of John: Puzzling Contextualization," *Exchange*, 9 (1980) 1–56.

11. For an excellent study of these "christologies," see M. M. Thomas, *The Acknowledged Christ of Indian Renaissance* (London: SCM Press, 1969) and S. J. Samartha, *The Hindu Response to the Unbound Christ* (Bangalore: Christian Institute for the Study of Religion and Society, 1974).

CHAPTER 7

1. Roy Preiswerk, "La rupture avec les conceptions actuelles du développement," in *Rélations interculturelles et développement* (Geneva, 1975), pp. 71–96.

2. R. C. Zaehner, *Foolishness to the Greeks* (Oxford: Clarendon Press, 1953), p. 7.

3. For a discussion on this matter, see *Buddhism in Ceylon and Studies on Religious Syncretism in Buddhist Countries*, H. Bechert, ed. (Göttingen: Vandenhoeck & Ruprecht, 1978), esp. part 3, pp. 146–339.

4. Rock Edict XIII of Asoka speaks of Buddhist missions to Syria. A complement to this is the Aramaic inscription found in eastern Afghanistan in 1969.

5. "Samāgama Sutta" of the *Majjhima Nikāya*.

6. See E. Conze, *Buddhism* (Oxford: Bruno Cassierer, 1953), pp. 64–65.

7. See Dulamzhavyn Dashzhamts, "Non-Capitalist Development and Religion," *World Marxist Review*, Dec. 1973, pp. 27–29.

8. For an exhaustive historical illustration, see *The Two Wheels of the Dhamma:*

Essays on Theravada Tradition in India and Ceylon, Bardwel L. Smith, ed. (Chambersburg, Pa.: American Academy of Religion, 1972).

9. News item "Militant Monks," in *Far Eastern Economic Review*, Sept. 30, 1977.

10. In "Cakkavattisīhanāda Suttanta" of the *Dīgha Nikāya*.

11. See Daniel L. Overmyer, "Folk-Buddhist Religion: Creation and Eschatology in Medieval China," *History of Religions*, 12 (1972) 42–70.

12. See Holmes Welch, *Buddhism Under Mao* (Cambridge, Mass.: Harvard University Press, 1972), pp.1–41, 340–63.

13. See *Karl Marx sulla religione*, Luciano Parinetto, ed. (Milan, 1972), pp. 511ff., referred to in *Church within Socialism*, Erich Weingärtner, ed. (IDOC International, Rome, 1976), p. 9.

14. The CBA was heard from again; see *China Talk*, 8/78, quoted in *LWF Marxism and China Study*, Information Letter, no. 23 (Sept. 1978), p. 5.

15. Parallel to CBA activities, there was, on the pro-Western side, a world conference called the World Buddhist Union whose political leanings could be guessed from the nonparticipation of mainland China, N. Vietnam, and N. Korea, and the presence of Taiwan and S. Vietnam (see *World Buddhism*, 19 [1970] 111). It regarded itself as the fourth world organization after the WFB, WBSS, and WBSC (ibid., 19 [1970] 136).

16. See *World Buddhism*, 18 (1970) 325, and 19 (1970) 17.

17. "Relevance of Buddhist Studies," *World Buddhism*, 21 (1972) 67ff.

18. Quoted in Charles Davis, *Christ and the World Religions* (New York: Herder & Herder, 1971), p. 21.

19. *Populorum Progressio*, no. 20.

20. See Edward Schillebeeckx, *God the Future of Man* (New York: Sheed & Ward, 1968), p. 54.

21. See Langdon Gilkey, *Religion and the Scientific Future* (New York: Harper & Row, 1970), pp. 76–77.

22. See *Populorum Progressio*, no. 20.

23. My study of healing ceremonies shows that demons associated with sickness are brought to the open and then eliminated; the Buddha then emerges as the Powerful One. His doctrine, well observed, is presented as the cure par excellence. The beliefs of the cosmic religions are continually purified and made to align with the metacosmic goal of perfection.

24. See Piero Gheddo, *Why Is the Third World Poor?* (Maryknoll, N.Y.: Orbis, 1973), pp. 30–37 and passim.

25. E. F. Schumacher, *Small is Beautiful: Economics as if People Mattered* (New York: Harper & Row, 1973).

26. See Weingärtner, *Church* (n. 13, above), p. 3.

27. See *Towards the Christian Revolution*, R. B. Y. Scott and G. Viastos, eds. (London: Gollancz, 1937), p. 104.

28. Mark Schoof, *Breakthrough: The Beginnings of the New Catholic Theology* (Dublin: Gill and Macmillan, 1970), p. 17.

29. Ibid., pp. 22–30.

30. It is observed (ibid., p. 26) that the new theology began by making the "whole life of the church" the locus of theological reflection, especially, *"the world in which this community* (of the church) *lived*, especially, *the world of contemporary philosophy"* (emphasis and parentheses added). The way *the world in which the church lived* is filtered into "the world of philosophy" would not escape Latin American criticism.

31. For a lucid exposition of this Latin American breakthrough, see Jon Sobrino, "El conocimiento teológico en la teología europea y latinoamericana," *Liberación y cautiverio: Debates en torno al método de la teología en América Latina* (Mexico City: Comité Organizador, 1975), pp. 177–207. For a concise summary of it, see Alfred T. Hennelly, "Theological Method: the Southern Exposure," *Theological Studies*, 38 (1977) 708–35.

32. "Conocimiento teológico," passim.

33. However, a relatively early example of a pioneering, and perhaps premature but certainly praiseworthy, attempt at a Christian assessment of the Marxist challenge can be found in *Towards the Christian Revolution* (n. 27, above).

34. According to the thesis put forward by Wolfhart Pannenberg in his *Theology and Philosophy of Science* (London: Darton, Longman & Todd, 1976), the main task of theology is to establish rationally the truth of theological propositions.

35. For a self-understanding of Catholic theology as a scientific pursuit, see Yves Congar, *A History of Theology* (Garden City, N.Y.: Doubleday, 1968), pp. 221ff.

36. Here Sobrino ("Conocimiento teológico," p. 201) quotes Moltmann. See Hennelly, "Theological Method," p. 721.

37. Hennelly, "Theological Method," pp. 710–713.

38. *Peking Review*, no. 47 (Nov. 24, 1978), p. 31; emphasis added.

39. See K. Malalgoda, *Buddhism in Sinhalese Society 1750–1900. A Study of Religious Revival and Change* (Berkeley: University of California Press, 1976), pp. 173–74.

40. Ibid., pp. 191–96.

41. See my "Western Christianity and Eastern Religions: A Theological Reading of Historical Encounters," *Dialogue*, 7 (1980) 49–85.

42. See Pannenberg, *Theology*, p.10.

43. *Nibbānabhimulhā paññā, saṃsārābhimukhā karunā.* For a lengthy excursus on the dialectics between *paññā* and *karunā*, see *Itv A* 1, 15–16, *Cp A*, 289–90, *Pm*, 192–93.

CHAPTER 8

1. Virginia Fabella, ed., *Asia's Struggle for Full Humanity* (Maryknoll, N.Y.: Orbis, 1980).

2. See chap. 7, above, passim.

3. Some aspects of the controversy can be gleaned from *Voices from the Third World*, June 1979; see also Fabella, *Asia's Struggle*, pp. 10–11, 165, 186.

4. See Pieris, "The Dynamics of the ATC. A Reply to Paul Caspersz," *Voices from the Third World*, (June 1979), pp. 23–28.

5. Albert Tevoedjre, *Poverty, Wealth of Peoples* (New York: Pergamon, 1978)—a rejoinder to Adam Smith's *Wealth of Nations*.

6. See, e.g., Luis A. Gomez de Souza, "Structures and Mechanisms of Domination in Capitalism," in *The Challenge of Basic Christian Communities*, Sergio Torres and John Eagleson, eds. (Maryknoll, N.Y.: Orbis, 1981), p. 16.

7. Gustavo Gutiérrez, "Irruption of the Poor in Latin America and the Christian Communities of the Common People," in Torres and Eagleson, *Challenge*, pp. 113–14.

8. Enrique Dussel, "Current Events in Latin America (1972–1980)," in Torres and Eagleson, *Challenge*, pp. 100–101.

9. See Juan Carlos Scannone, "Theology, Popular Culture and Discernment," in *Frontiers of Theology in Latin America*, Rosino Gibellini, ed. (Maryknoll, N.Y.: Orbis, 1979), p. 221.

10. See José Miranda, *Being and the Messiah: The Message of St. John* (Maryknoll, N.Y.: Orbis, 1977), pp. 39–42 and passim.

11. Jon Sobrino, *Christology at the Crossroads* (Maryknoll, N.Y.: Orbis, 1978), pp. 275ff.

12. This trend is not restricted to the Philippines. In the Indian group that discussed my Wennappuwa EATWOT conference paper in Bangalore immediately after the conference, many of the participants shared this conviction.

13. Edward Schillebeeckx, *God the Future of Man* (New York: Sheed & Ward, 1968), pp. 57–58.

14. Gerhard Kittel, *Theological Dictionary of the New Testament* (Grand Rapids: Eerdmans, 1971), vol. 2, p. 20; vol. 3, pp. 123–38; vol. 3, pp. 155ff., 175, 181.

15. See esp. Antonio Pérez-Esclarín, *Atheism and Liberation* (Maryknoll, N.Y.: Orbis, 1978), pp. 160–61.

16. Diane Paul, " 'In the Interest of Civilization': Marxist Views of Race and Culture in the Nineteenth Century," *Journal of the History of Ideas*, 42 (1981)138–39.

17. Lelio Basso, "La via non-capitalistica al socialismo," in *Imperialismo e Rivoluzione Socialista nel Terzo Mondo*, S. Amin et al., eds. (Milan: Franco Angeli, 1979), pp. 9–31.

18. See "A Leap across Centuries" (team report on Mongolia on the sixtieth anniversary of the Revolution), *World Marxist Review*, 24 (1981) 49–54.

19. See Jean Ziegler, "Elementi di una teoria sulle società socialiste precapitaliste," in Amin, *Imperialismo*, p. 42.

20. See Patric Chabal, "The Social and Political Thought of Amilcar Cabral: A Reassessment," *Journal of Modern African Studies*, 19 (1981) 31–56.

21. See P. G. Casanova, "Le minoranze etniche in America Latina: dal sottosviluppo al socialismo," in Amin, *Imperialismo*, p. 96.

22. See John Swetman, "Class-based and Community-based Ritual Organization in Latin America," *Ethnology*, 17 (1978) 425–38.

23. At the Cartagena CELAM meeting (July 1980) the church was invited to study, defend, and foster Afro-American cultural values; see *Misiones Extranjeras*, 61–62 (1981) 217.

24. See R. R. Burgoa, "Clase y raza en los Andes," *Misiones Extranjeras*, 61–62 (1981) 269ff.

25. See Casanova, "Minoranze," p. 118.

26. The Soviets are accused of russifying and westernizing Asians in the U.S.S.R., and Soviet apologetics does not fully answer these charges; see Z. S. Chertina, "The Bourgeois Theory of Modernization and the Real Development of the Peoples of Soviet Central Asia," *Soviet Review,* 22 (1981) 77–78.

27. Torres and Eagleson, *Challenge*, pp. 5, 15–16, 42–45, 234.

28. For an extensive treatment of these Indian christologies, see M. M. Thomas, *The Acknowledged Christ of the Indian Renaissance* (London: SCM Press, 1969), and S. J. Samartha, *The Hindu Response to the Unbound Christ* (Madras: CLS, 1974).

29. The most popular statement of this thesis at the time was that of A. T. Van Leeuwen, *Christianity in World History: The Meeting of Faiths of East and West* (London: Eddinburgh House, 1964). It is taken up also by Piero Gheddo, *Why is the Third World Poor?* (Maryknoll, N.Y.: Orbis, 1973), esp. pp. 30–37 and passim.

30. See the chapter on "Buddhist Economics" in E. F. Schumacher, *Small is Beautiful: Economics as if People Mattered* (London and New York: Harper & Row, 1973); see also K. Ishwaran, *"Bhakti* Tradition and Modernization: The Case for *Lingayatism,"* *Journal of Asian and African Studies*, 15 (1980) 72–82.

31. A delicate and comprehensive critique, representative of this period, is that of Denis Goulet, "On the Goals of Development," *Cross Currents*, 18 (1968) 387–405.

32. Namely, in chap. 4, above.

33. For a forceful exposition of this thesis, see E. T. Jacob-Pandian, "Anthropological Fieldwork, Empathy and the Crisis of the Apocalyptic Man," *Man in India*, 55 (1975) 281–97; see also Epeli Han'ofa, "Anthropology and Pacific Islanders," *Man in India*, 55 (1975) 57–66.

34. See E. E. Evans-Pritchard, "Religion and the Anthropologists," *Practical Anthropology*, 19 (1972) 193, 205, quoted in Claud E. Stipe, "The Role of Religion in Cultural Change," *Christian Scholar's Review*, 10 (1981) 120.

35. Stipe, "Role of Religion," pp. 117ff.

36. F. Sierksma, *Current Anthropology*, 6 (1965) 455.

37. See Vittorro Lanternari, *The Religion of the Oppressed: A Study of Modern Messianic Cults* (New York: Mentor, 1963), p. 312.

38. See Stipe, "The Role of Religion," p. 121; for concrete examples, see pp. 124–28. See also Ishwaran, "*Bhakti* Tradition," pp. 80–82.

39. Chap. 7, above, pp. 70–71.

40. Ibid., pp. 71–72.

41. Ibid., p. 73.

42. Ibid., pp. 71–72.

43. Ibid., p. 72.

44. For some case studies, see Stipe, "Role of Religion," pp. 124–28.

45. See G. H. Jansen, *Militant Islam* (New York: Harper & Row, 1979), pp. 54–56. Though tendentious, these pages are an eye-opener.

46. Quoted in James H. Billington, "Christianity in USSR," *Theology Today*, 36 (1980) 207.

47. Quoted in CALA *News Letter*, 8 (1981) 1.

48. Chabal, "Social and Political Thought of Amilcar Cabral," pp. 42–54.

49. Ziegler, "Elementi," pp. 38–39.

50. Ibid., p. 36.

51. Sergio Vieira, "Stages of Fundamental Changes," *World Marxist Review*, Jan. 1981, pp. 15–20.

52. Ibid., p. 15. Unlike Belgium, France, and Britain, Portugal did not accumulate capital but wasted it on aristocratic pageantry, except during the last hundred years, so that it could not have maintained the metropolis and Portuguese settlers in colonial territories had it given them independence.

53. Ibid., p. 17.

54. Jansen, *Militant Islam*, chaps. 3 and 4.

55. From a manuscript version of a lecture by Dr. Eqbal Ahmed at the Riverside Church in New York, Jan. 20, 1980.

56. See Margaret Chatterjee, "The Concept of Multiple Allegiance: A Hypothesis Concerning the Contemporary Indian Spectrum," *Man in India*, 56 (1976) 123–33.

57. Bachandra Nemade, "The Revolt of the Underprivileged," *Journal of Asian and African Studies*, 15 (1980) 113.

58. Ibid., pp. 113–23.

59. See Jayashree Gokhale-Turner, "Bhakti or Vidroha: Continuity and Change in Dalit Sahitya," *Journal of Asian and African Studies*, 15 (1980) 29–42.

60. Ibid., pp. 37–39.

61. For a case study on feudalization of tribal societies, see Jaganath Pathy, "Political Economy of Kandha Land," *Man in India*, 56 (1976) 1–36.

62. See K. D. Gangrade, "Social Mobility in India: A Study in Depressed Classes," *Man in India*, 55 (1975) 258 and 278, n. 19.

63. See Gail Omvedt, "Adivasis and Modes of Production in India," *Bulletin of Concerned Asian Scholars*, 12 (1980) 15–22. See also Gautama Bhadra, "The Kuki (?) Uprising (1917–1919): Its Causes and Nature," *Man in India*, 55 (1975)10–58.

64. See Paul Demiéville, "Le bouddhisme et la guerre," in *Mélange* (Paris, 1957), vol. 1, pp. 375–84.

65. See Charles F. Keyes, "Political Crisis and Militant Buddhism in Contemporary Thailand," in *Religion and Legitimation of Power in Thailand*, Bardwel Smith, ed. (Chambersburg, Pa.: Anima, 1978), p. 160.

66. For an excellent treatment of this history, see E. Sarkisyanz, *The Buddhist Backgrounds of the Burmese Revolutions* (The Hague: Nijhoff, 1965).

67. See Demiéville, "Bouddhisme," pp. 357–68; see also Daniel L. Overmyer, "Folk-Buddhist Religion: Creation and Eschatology in Medieval China," *History of Religions*, 12 (1972) 42–70.

68. Chap. 7, above, p. 80.

69. See K. Zaradov, "The Environmental Movement and the Communists: The Political Class Approach," *World Marxist Review*, 24 (1981) 50–53.

70. See Chertina, "Bourgeois Theory" (n. 26, above), p. 69.

71. Theodore Reik, *Of Love and Lust* (New York and Toronto: Bantam, 1967), p. 470.

72. See chap. 4, above.

73. See Jacob-Pandian, "Anthropological Fieldwork" (n. 33, above).

CHAPTER 9

1. Sacred Congregation for Doctrine and Faith, *Instruction on Certain Aspects of the "Theology of Liberation"* (Vatican City, 1984), III/4. It is to this source that I refer when I use such titles as "the Roman document," "the Roman Instruction," "the Ratzinger document," etc.

2. Ibid.

3. E.g., see chap. 7, above.

4. E.g., the prolonged debate among Third World theologians on inculturation and liberation since 1979; see *Voices from the Third World*, June 1979.

5. See Carolyn Osiek, "Slavery in the New Testament World," *Bible Today* (1984) 151ff.

6. *Instruction*, Introduction IV/2 and passim.

7. Ph. I. André-Vincent, "Les 'théologies de la libération,' " *Nouvelle Revue Théologique*, 98 (1976) 121–22.

8. See Gervase Corcoran, "Slavery in the New Testament," part 2, *Milltown Studies* (Dublin), 6 (1980) 75–77.

9. James A. Brundage, "Prostitution in the Medieval Canon Law," *Signs: Journal of Women in Culture and Society*, I (1976) 825ff.

10. See S. Rajamanickam, *The First Oriental Scholar* (Tirunelveli: De Nobili Research Institute, 1972), pp. 61–63. This is the most reliable and informative work on De Nobili available today.

11. Anne Yarbrough, "Christianization in the Fourth Century: The Example of the Roman Women," *Church History*, 45 (1976) 149ff.

12. Max L. Stackhouse, "Some Intellectual and Social Roots of Modern Human

Rights Ideas," *Journal of the Scientific Study of Religions*, 20 (1981) 301.

13. Yarbrough, "Christianization," p. 157.

14. Peter R. L. Brown, *Augustine of Hippo. A Biography* (London: Faber, 1967), p. 115, quoted in Yarbrough, "Christianization," p. 157.

15. Ibid.

16. This instruction issued by the Propaganda Fide to the (French) vicars apostolic in the Far-Eastern missions in 1659 is alleged by Massimo Marocchi to be a historical breakthrough in that it rejects the medieval association of spiritual authority and temporal powers, and distances itself from the Jesuit method of conversion "from top to bottom." See *Colonialismo, cristianesimo e culture extraeuropee* (Milan: Jaca Book, 1981), p. 54. This is indeed a forced interpretation of the instruction, which nowhere advocates a bottom-to-top method of missionary involvement. I hope later to analyze the motivation behind this document and verify its alleged modernity.

17. Juan María Lozano, *Discipleship. Towards an Understanding of Religious Life* (Chicago: Claretian Press, 1980), pp. 183–85.

18. See chap. 2, above.

19. For a short excursus on this theory, see Aloysius Pieris, "Political Vision of the Buddhists," *Dialogue* (Colombo), 11 (1984) 6ff.; see also "Monastic Poverty in the Asian Setting," *Dialogue*, 8 (1980) 104ff.

20. Lozano, *Discipleship*, p. 189.

21. George M. Soares-Prabhu, "Class in the Bible: The Biblical Poor, a Social Class?," *Vidyajyoti*, 49 (1985) 320–46.

22. Ibid., p. 327.

23. Ibid., pp. 345–46, italics added.

24. *Asia's Struggle for Full Humanity*, Virginia Fabella, ed. (Maryknoll, N.Y.: Orbis, 1980).

25. See chap. 8, above, pp. 97–98, 100–106.

Publications in Western Languages by Aloysius Pieris, S.J.

ARTICLES
(in chronological order)

"Liturgy and Dialogue with Buddhism: An Experiment," *Dialogue* (Colombo), o.s. 15 (1968) 1–16.

"Liturgy in God's World," *Outlook* (Colombo), 2 (1969) 10–12.

"The Liturgy and the 'New Breed,' " *Logos* (Colombo), 9 (1968) 35–43. Reprinted: *Quest*, 4 (1969) 45–53; *Liturgical Arts*, 38 (1969) 2ff.

"The Indian Rite Controversy," *Worship*, 43 (1969) 219–24.

"The Church, the Kingdom, and the Other Religions," *Dialogue*, o.s. 22 (1970) 3–7. Reprinted: *Tjurunga* (Australia), 11 (1976) 73–84; *Current Documentation* (Rome), 4 (1976) 1–9.

"From Mary of Nazareth to a Church in Crisis," *Outlook*, 3 (1970) 5–7, 14.

"Diplomacy? The Church Cannot Stomach It," *Outlook*, 3 (1970) 5–8.

"From Lilies to Roses," *Outlook*, 3 (1970) 6–11.

"Confusion and Rebellion," *Outlook*, 4 (1971) 5–9.

"Catholic Education and the Rehabilitation of the Misguided," *Outlook*, 4 (1971) 8–12.

"Some Christian Reflections on Buddhism and Secularisation in Ceylon," *Dialogue*, o.s. 24 (1972) 3–8.

"A Mass for Republic Day," *Outlook*, 5 (1972) 5–12.

"Buddhism as Doctrine, Institution, and Experience," *Dialogue*, o.s. 27–28 (1973) 3–7.

"Buddhist Christian Encounter I," *Dialogue*, o.s. 27–28 (1973) 18ff.

"Religion, Politics and Jesus Christ," *Outlook*, 6 (1973) 1–6.

"Fringe Groups and the Dialectics of Church Renewal," *Outlook*, 6 (1973) 9–13.

"Monkhood: Some Elementary Facts About Its Origin and Its Place in a Buddhist-Christian Dialogue," *Dialogue*, n.s. 1 (1974) 4–10. Reprinted: *Tjurunga*, 10 (1975) 67–74.

"Discussion on Nationalism, Politics and the Clergy," *Dialogue*, n.s. 1 (1974) 80–83.

"Did Jesus Die in Kashmir?" *Dialogue*, n.s. 1 (1974) 27f.

"The Legitimacy and the Limitations of the Academic Approach to Inter-Faith Dialogue," *Dialogue*, n.s. 1 (1974) 39–43. Reprinted: "The Academic Approach to Inter-Faith Dialogue," in *Toward World Community*, S.J. Samartha, ed., Geneva, WCC, 1975, pp. 146–48; *The Month*, 14 (1981) 147–48, 180.

"God-Talk and God-Experience in a Christian Perspective," *Dialogue*, 2 (1975) 116–28.

"Buddhist Christian Dialogue in Sri Lanka," *Impact* (Manila), 11 (1976) 158–61.

"The Zen-Christian Dialogue in Japan. The First Impressions of a Sri Lankan Christian," *Dialogue*, 3 (1976) 107–12.

"Contemporary Ecumenism and Asia's Search for Christ," in *Towards a "Dialogue of Life." Ecumenism in the Asian Context*, P. De Achutegui, ed. (Card. Bea Studies, IV), Manila, 1976, 154–74. Reprinted: *Teaching All Nations* (Manila), 13 (1976) 154–74;

Misiones Extranjeras (Madrid), 31 (1976) 14–32; *Outlook,* 8 (1976) 1–4; *The Month,* 11 (1978) 4–9; "Ökumenismus angesichts der Suche Asiens nach Christus," *Una Sancta,* 34 (1979) 319–32.

"The Spirituality of the Buddhist Monk in Sri Lanka," *Inter Fratres* (Fabriano), 27 (1977) 121–32. Reprinted: "La spiritualità del monaco buddhista nel Sri Lanka," in *Il monachesimo nel terzo mondo,* Rome, Paoline, 1979, pp. 190–203; *Tjurunga,* 17 (1979) 31–48; "Le moine bouddhiste à Sri Lanka. Sa spiritualité et sa mission," *Bulletin de l'A.I.M.* (Vanves), 27 (1980) 56–69.

"The Workers' Mass at a Factory," *Christian Workers' Fellowship* (Colombo), 1977, pp. 107–12.

"Doctrinal, Legal and Cultural Factors in Buddhist-Christian Mixed Marriages," *Dialogue,* 5 (1978) 91–107. Summary in *Theologie im Kontext* (Aachen), 0 (1979) 56.

"The Colophon to the Paramattamanjusa and the Discussion on the Date of Acariya Dhammapala," in *Buddhism in Ceylon and Studies on Religious Syncretism in Buddhist Countries,* H. Bechert, ed. (Symposien zur Buddhismusforschung, I), Göttingen, 1978, pp. 61–77.

"Towards an Asian Theology of Liberation: Some Religio-cultural Guidelines," *Dialogue,* 6 (1979) 29–52. Reprinted: *The Month,* 12 (1979) 148–59; *Vidyajyoti* (Delhi), 43 (1979) 261–84; *Zeitschrift für Missionswissenschaft und Religionswissenschaft,* 63 (1979) 161–82; *East Asian Pastoral Review,* 16 (1979) 206–30; *Logos* (Colombo), 19 (1980) 49–72; *Misiones Extranjeras,* 56 (1980) 155–78; *Eglise et Mission* (Brussels), 219 (1980) 10–28; *Monchanin* (Montreal), 13 (1980) 3–25; *Asia's Struggle for Full Humanity,* Virginia Fabella, ed., Maryknoll, N.Y., Orbis, 1980, pp. 75–95; *Living Theology in Asia,* John C. England, ed., London, SCM, 1981, pp. 171–76. Summary in *Theologie im Kontext,* 1 (1980) 93.

✓ "The Dynamics of the ATC [Asian Theological Conference]: A Reply to the Editor of Satyodaya," *Voices of the Third World,* 2 (1979) 23–29. Reprinted: *Logos,* 20 (1981) 73–78.

"Das Christentum des Westens und die Religionen des Ostens. Ein theologischer Vortrag über historische Begegnungen," in *Theologie in der Dritten Welt,* Evangelisches Missionswerk, Hamburg, 1979, pp. 4–39. Revised and reprinted: "Western Christianity and Eastern Religions," *Cistercian Studies,* 15 (1980) 50–66, 150–71. Reprinted: "Western Christianity and Asian Buddhism: A Theological Reading of Historical Encounters," *Dialogue,* 7 (1980) 49–85. Summary in *Theologie im Kontext,* 2 (1981) 114.

"The Notions of Citta, Atta and Attabhava in the Pali Exegetical Writings," in *Buddhist Studies in Honour of Walpola Rahula,* London, Fraser, 1980, pp. 213–22.

"Monastic Poverty in the Asian Setting," *Dialogue,* 7 (1980) 104–18. Reprinted: *Tjurunga,* 26 (1984) 5–16. Extract in "Les dimensions de la pauvreté volontaire," *Mission de l'Eglise* (Paris), 59 (1983) 36–40. Summary in *Theologie im Kontext,* 3 (1982) 120.

"Church Development in a Multireligious Sri Lanka," *SEDEC Bulletin* (Colombo), 1981, pp. 52–56.

"Jesus' Hands that Break the Bread," in *Souvenir of the Eucharistic Congress Held at Kandy,* Th. A. Pieris, ed., Kandy, 1981, pp. 57–59.

"Mission of the Local Church in Relation to Other Major Religious Traditions," *SEDOS Bulletin* (Rome), 5–7 (1982) 92–96, 103–9, 123–27. Reprinted: *Misiones Extranjeras,* 71 (1982) 349–68; *The Month,* 15 (1982) 81–90; *CTC Bulletin* (Singapore), 4 (1983) 30–42; *Voices from the Third World,* 8 (1985) 105–26; *Mission in*

Dialogue, M. Mott and J. Lang, eds., Maryknoll, N.Y., Orbis, 1982, pp. 426–41. Summary in *Theologie im Kontext,* 4 (1983) 93.

"Speaking of the Son of God in Non-Christian Cultures, e.g., in Asia," *Concilium,* 153 (1982), 206–11.

"The Place of Non-Christian Religions and Cultures in the Evolution of a Third-World Theology," *CTC Bulletin,* 3 (1982) 43–61. Reprinted: "Der Ort der nichtchristlichen Religionen in der Entwicklung einer Theologie der Dritten Welt," *Zeitschrift für Missionswissenschaft und Religionswissenschaft,* 66 (1982) 241–70, *Vidyajyoti,* 46 (1982) 158–70, 227–45; *East Asian Pastoral Review,* 19 (1982) 5–33; *Misiones Extranjeras,* 72 (1982) 463–94; *Irruption of the Third World: Challenge to Theology,* Virginia Fabella and Sergio Torres, eds. (Maryknoll, N.Y., Orbis, 1983), pp. 113–39. Summary in *Theologie im Kontext,* 4 (1983) 107.

"Rev. Dr. Lynn A. De Silva—A Tribute," *Supplement to Dialogue,* 9 (1982) 1–8.

The Buddhist Worldview and the Christian Kerygma, Teape Wescott Lectures, delivered at the University of Cambridge, England, October 1982. To be published.

"La espiritualidad en una perspectiva de liberación," in *Vida y Reflexión,* Lima, 1983, pp. 179–99. Reprinted: "Spirituality in a Liberation Perspective," *East Asian Pastoral Review,* 20 (1983) 139–50; *The Month,* 16 (1983) 118–24; *Logos,* 24 (1985) 42–62. Summary in *Theologie im Kontext,* 5 (1984) 128; 7 (1986) 103.

"Ideology and Religion: Some Debatable Points," *Dialogue,* 10 (1983) 31–41. Reprinted: *Voices from the Third World,* 8 (1985) 74–83.

"The Cult of the Sacred Tooth Relic—Its Origin and Meaning," *Dialogue,* 10 (1983) 63–72.

"Dom Leo Nanayakkara: Bishop and Monk," *Tjurunga,* 25 (1983) 73–79.

"The Political Vision of the Buddhists," *Dialogue,* 11 (1984) 6–14.

"To Be Poor as Jesus Was Poor?" *The Way* (London), 24 (1984) 186–97.

"L'Asie non sémitique face aux modèles occidentaux d'inculturation," *Lumière et Vie,* 33 (1984) 50–62. Reprinted: "Asien: Welches Inkulturationsmodell?" *Orientierung,* 49 (1985) 102–6; "Western Models of Inculturation: How Far Are They Applicable in Non-Semitic Asia?" *East Asian Pastoral Review,* 22 (1985) 116–24; *Vidyajyoti,* 435–45; *The Month* 19 (1986) 83–87. Summary, "Der Ruf Asiens zur Welkirche," in *Christ in der Gegenwart* (Freiburg) 37 (1985) 211f.

"Buddhism and Marxism in Dialogue: A Comment on Dr. Dharmasiri's Paper," *Dialogue,* 12 (1985) 68–86.

"A Theology of Liberation in the Asian Churhes?" *Japan Missionary Bulletin* (Tokyo), 40 (1986) 165–79. Reprinted: *The Month,* 19 (1986) 148–59; *Vidyajyoti,* 50 (1986) 330–51; *Misiones Extranjeras,* 95 (1986) 348–66; *East Asian Pastoral Review,* 23 (1986) 117-37. CTC Bulletin (Singapore), 6 (1986) 1–12.

"Buddhism as a Challenge for Christians," *Concilium,* 183 (1986) 40–44.

Theologie der Befreiung in Asien (Theologie der Dritten Welt, 9) Freiburg/Basel/Vienna, Herder, 1986, 270 pp.

"The Buddha and the Christ: Mediators of Liberation," in *The Myth of Christian Uniqueness: Toward a Pluralistic Theology of Religions,* John Hick and Paul F. Knitter, eds., Maryknoll, N.Y., Orbis, 1987, pp. 162–77.

"Christentum und Buddhismus im Dialog aus der Mitte ihrer Traditionen," in *Dialog aus der Mitte christlicher Theologie,* A. Bsteh, ed., Mödling, St. Gabriel, 1987, pp. 131–78.

"Christianity and Buddhism in Core-to-Core Dialogue," *Cross Currents,* 37 (1987) 47–75. Also in *Vidyajyoti,* October 1987, pp. 46–83; November 1987, pp. 575–88.

REVIEWS AND INTRODUCTIONS

"Ecumenism Today," in *Ceylon Churchman* (Colombo), 67 (1971) 51f.

"Did Jesus Come to India to Study Buddhism?" *Dialogue*, 1 (1974) 57–60.

"Monkhood: Sociological Analysis and Theological Perspectives," *Dialogue*, 1 (1974) 93–99.

"Mutual Exposure of Religions," *Dialogue*, 1 (1975) 45–46.

"A Buddhist Critique and a Christian Response," *Dialogue*, 2 (1975) 83–85.

"World Buddhism and Dialogue," *Dialogue*, 3 (1976) 85–87.

"Religion and Politics in Sri Lanka: The Role of the Sinhala Monk," *Dialogue*, 3 (1976) 113–16.

"What the Secular Has Put Together, Let No Religion Put Asunder," *Dialogue*, 5 (1978) 57f.

"Buddhist Socialism," *Lanka Guardian* (Colombo), 2 (1979) 17f. Reprinted: *Devasarana Development Centre*, Colombo, 1982, pp. 24f.

"The Monastic Conference at Kandy on Asian Poverty," *Dialogue*, 7 (1980) 97f.

"Conversion, Controversy and Conversation," *Dialogue*, 9 (1982) 1f.

"How Catholic is the Catholic's View of God, Man and the Universe?" *Dialogue*, 9 (1982) 122f.

"Asiens Kampf um volle Menschlichkeit—unterwegs zu einer relevanten Theologie," Introduction to *Herausgefordert durch die Armen. Dokumente der ökumenischen Vereinigung von Dritte-Welt-Theologen 1976-1983* (Theologie der Dritten Welt, 4), Freiburg /Basel/ Vienna, Herder, 1983, pp. 63–67.

"Buddhist Honours for Christian Priests," *Dialogue*, 10 (1983) 1–3.

"The Solitary Ascetic in Hindu and Buddhist Traditions," *Dialogue*, 10 (1983) 47–55.

STUDIES ON ALOYSIUS PIERIS

Arnulf Camps, "Salvation bij Aloysius Pieris, S.J., Sri Lanka," in *Heil voor deze Wereld* (Studies aangeboden aan prof. dr. A. G. Honig, Jr.), Kampen, J.H.Kok, 1984, pp. 63–71.

N. Abeyasingha, *The Radical Tradition: The Changing Shape of Theological Reflection in Sri Lanka*, Colombo, The Ecumenical Institute, 1985, pp. 126–32.

Jos Demon, "Aloysius Pieris: een 'boeddhistisch' Jezuiet. Een zelfgetuigenis," in *Verwijlen onder de Bodhi-boom,* Dorsthorst-Fritschy-Heijke, eds., Bolsward, 1985, pp. 17–36.

Ulrich Dornberg, "Kontextuelle Theologie in Sri Lanka" (M. A. dissertation under Prof. J. B. Metz), Münster, 1985, xvii + 271 pp.

Marinus Huijbregts, "Dopen in the Jordaan van Azie" (Th.D. dissertation under Prof. A. Camps), Nijmegen, 1986, iii + 113pp.

Index